LEADERSHIP SKILLS FOR WOMEN

Communication Skills

New Hope
Birmingham, Alabama

HARRIET HARRAL

Published by:
New Hope
P.O. Box 12065
Birmingham, AL 35202-2065

Cover illustration by Cathy Robbins

Dewey Decimal classification:153.6

Subject Headings: WOMEN—PSYCHOLOGY
                     WOMEN—BIBLICAL TEACHING
                     WOMEN IN THE BIBLE
                     COMMUNICATION
                     HUMAN RELATIONS

Series: Leadership Skills for Women

ISBN: 1-56309-104-6

N943115•0594•7.5M1

Church Study Course number 03386

Contents

"You cannot not communicate."

This axiom of communication provides incentive enough for any leader to spend some time studying communication! If we cannot *not* communicate, then we must be communicating all the time. That can be a frightening thought! What myriad messages am I sending to you? What are the multitude of meanings that you are mulling over as you begin reading this book? What will remain with you? What will you forget even as you turn the page? The answers to these questions are as varied as the readers of this book. That is why studying communication is so complex and so rewarding, so frustrating and so much fun, so immediate and so far-reaching.

This book will not answer all your questions. It will not make you an expert communicator. My prayer as its author is that it will give you some new ideas and reinforce some old ones. I hope it will alert you to some pitfalls and some opportunities. My goal is to provide you with a ready resource to point out patterns, assist your planning as a leader, and open windows of understanding between you and those with whom you work in the cause of Christ.

In this book you will meet and/or become better acquainted with Biblical women who demonstrate to us some critical communication skills needed by leaders. They give evidence that women have been in roles of leadership for centuries. They can guide us as we seek to fulfill our responsibilities today.

Each chapter deals with one of the particular communication skills needed by a leader. Included in each chapter is a woman role model, skill explanation, skill assessment, skill practice, and skill evaluation.

This format was chosen because it tracks the way we learn a new skill. First, we need to see the skill modeled. Next, it needs to be explained. Third, we need to try it and assess our own level of competence at the skill. Fourth, we practice to improve our skill, and finally, we evaluate how we are doing as we apply the skill to actual situations.

The chapter topics were chosen carefully. As you prepare for your study, review this chapter by chapter synopsis.

• *Chapter 1. Communication: What It Is and How It Works.* Understanding the processes of communication gives us an opportunity to avoid misunderstandings.

• *Chapter 2. Leadership: What It Is and How We Can Get Better at It.* Leadership is not inherent; it is a set of skills which can be learned. You can improve your leadership skills.

• *Chapter 3. Interpersonal Communication: Perception Is Reality.* The other person is always your primary consideration when you want effective communication. How can you help them understand?

• *Chapter 4. Listening: The Creative Art.* Paying attention to others is the most important thing you can do to improve communication. Truly, listening is an art.

• *Chapter 5. Nonverbal Messages: The Art of Unspoken Communication.* By far the greatest percentage of meaning is nonverbal; how can you better communicate without words?

• *Chapter 6. Public Presentations: The Confident Speaker.* Public speaking, the most prominent fear among adults, can become a tool you will enjoy using.

• *Chapter 7. The Message: Making It Meaningful.* How can you construct your messages to maximize the chances that you will be understood?

• *Chapter 8. Women of God: Leaders and Communicators.* The charge is given to you. How will you use this information?

My hope is that this book will help you approach the tasks of leadership with more confidence. A major theme in the book is that an effective communicator always focuses on the receiver, demonstrating an attitude consistent with effective Christianity. Our focus is to lead in such a way that other Christians may see Christ in our behavior, and in so doing, join in missions efforts to win the lost to Him.

CHAPTER 1

Communication: What It Is and How It Works

Abigail, an intelligent woman, was the wife of Nabal, a wealthy man who was surly and mean. At one time, Nabal's shepherds spent time at Carmel under David's protection. Some time later, David and his men arrived in Nabal's territory during the festive time of sheep shearing. Approaching Nabal with greetings, they asked for food. Afraid his servants would leave if he gave away resources, Nabal scornfully refused them and sent them away. David was furious and swore he would kill every male in the household of Nabal.

One of Abigail's servants ran to warn her of the danger from David and explained that David's people had been very kind to them. Abigail immediately gathered donkey-loads of bread, wine, fruit, and grain. Without telling Nabal, she and her servants travelled to David's camp.

As soon as Abigail saw David, she fell to the ground and apologized for her husband's actions. She then acknowledged David's destiny as king and predicted a great future for him. She argued that in his time of success, David would not want on his conscience the staggering burden of needless bloodshed.

Persuaded by Abigail, David thanked her for saving him from the burden of vengefulness. Abigail went home and told Nabal what she had done. His heart failed, and he soon died. When David heard of this, he sent for Abigail to become his wife (based on 1 Sam. 25).

Abigail was an excellent communicator. She models for us

the most effective approach we can take to understand and be understood. And isn't that what communication is all about? It certainly is what the rest of this book is about!

In order to communicate effectively as leaders, we need to understand the process of communication. It's interesting that something as integral to our lives as the way we communicate is something that we take for granted. That seems to be true of many of the things which are most important to us. We forget to consciously work at being healthy, at being a family and being a friend, at being Christian; yet our ability to be our best at dealing with ourselves, with others, and with God is at the heart of good communication.

This book is designed to help you consciously think about communication and how it influences your relationships and ability to be a good leader. In order to do that, it is important to understand the basic process of communication. *Ethical communication*, a term used in the book, demonstrates respect and concern for all involved. The communication transaction is not manipulative or overpowering. Those involved should be concerned that the other persons involved understand meaning and intent.

True communication requires that we accept others' freedom of choice. If we respect their free choice-making capability, we demonstrate our respect for them as individuals. In other words, our attitudes toward others in the communication situation are more significant than content of the message. This fundamental standard for our communication as leaders is also our Christian responsibility.

What does being a choice-maker mean? Whenever a person is capable of doing something, and is also capable of not doing it, the person has a choice. The more options there are to choose from, the more freedom of choice a person has. When all options are equally accessible, a person has maximum freedom of choice.

Obviously, we frequently have less than maximum freedom of choice. Physical conditions, past experiences, habits, values, other people, lack of imagination, and a host of other things may restrict the number of options we have to choose from. They may also restrict the accessibility, desirability, or probability of choosing any one of the options.

I remember hearing a conversation my four-year-old son,

Huard, had with a five-year-old neighbor. Huard asked Katie to come over to play. She said she couldn't because she already had a friend playing at her house, but she invited Huard to join them. Huard kept insisting that Katie come to our house. She finally said, "Huard, that's just not one of the options. You have to come over here or just not play with me." Katie realized that neither she nor Huard had full freedom of choice. Huard felt the constraints of a situation requiring a choice. He didn't go play, but it was not a choice he wanted to make.

Our choices range, then, from basic ones such as Hamlet's "to be or not to be" to such questions as *What will I wear today?* We choose whether to speak or not to speak; how to say what we choose to say; to laugh, scorn, cry, or applaud responses to what we say. Sometimes all the options are desirable, and we want them all. Sometimes all the options seem undesirable, and we want to choose not to choose. Even that is a choice.

To be honest, then, we recognize choice-making as a fundamental exercise of humanity. The recognition is also a practical one. In a communication situation we recognize the other person as a free choice-maker, and accept that person's choice. Paul Keller and Charles Brown have identified at least four benefits from this recognition.

1. The more freedom of choice a person has, the more information is conveyed by the choice. If you freely choose to behave in a friendly way toward me, I can attribute more significance to your friendship than if your job, role, or position requires you to be friendly toward me.

2. A freely made choice carries more commitment than does a forced or tricked choice. Consider the dropout rate among converts to Christianity who made their decision on an emotional high because they were essentially tricked or manipulated by the circumstances.

3. Our recognition of the other person's choice conveys that we have respect for the individual.

4. As we recognize the other person's freedom of choice, we reward or reinforce the other person for taking the responsibility of making choices.

Before I move on to some applications of this principle, I want to issue a warning. An emphasis on respecting another's choice should not imply a lack of personal standards or commitment. At times we must take a stand. Freedom of choice is a paradox of living with both uncertainty and certainty, keeping an open mind about some issues while making up your mind about others. As leaders trying to exercise honest communication, we will feel the pull of the poles.

Models of Communication

The following models of communication illustrate three distinct attitudes people have about communication and how they relate to each other as choice-makers. Each of these models is exemplified in the story of Abigail.

•The Action (or One-Way) Model of Communication. The first attitude we often see demonstrated about communication says essentially that communication comes from the communicator. It places the entire responsibility for the success of communication on the person sending a message. The model was developed in the 1940s and includes these major elements:

In this model, communication is like an inoculation. Someone has an idea, squeezes it out through some medium or channel, and squirts it into the receiver. Communication would certainly be easy if it worked that way!

Some statements indicating an action orientation toward communication are:

I'm sure they understood me; I repeated my instructions three times.

She just never makes any sense; I turn her off whenever she starts talking.

I've got a great speech! It works anywhere.

I'm a failure; no one ever listens to me.

This philosophy indicates that if a misunderstanding occurs, it must be because the sender didn't say the message right, didn't package her meaning well, or made some kind of mistake. This is the philosophy at work when people are terrified of giving a speech; they feel that the success of the situation depends entirely on them.

This kind of thinking about communication is followed by the idea that the audience, or the receiver, plays no part in the communication process. Their thoughts, feelings, attitudes, and reactions are irrelevant. When the sender takes all the responsibility for the communication, all of the sender's attention is focused on self; there is no attention being given to the reaction or feedback of the receivers.

Nabal exemplifies a one-way attitude toward communication. He was interested only in his own needs and attitudes; he took no time to weigh how his audience, David's men, might react. He worried about his servants deserting him if he gave food away, but he never stopped to think that they might be distressed at the danger he put them in by making David angry.

A one-way attitude toward communication is self-centered, short-sighted, and inaccurate.

Skill Assessment: One-Way Communication

1. List three examples of treating communication as if it were one-way. _____

_____

2. How do you feel when you are in a situation in which the other person treats communication as all one-way? _____

_____

3. Think of a time when you behaved as if communication were just one-way. What happened? How did you feel? How did the other person feel? _____

_____

_____

Skill Practice: Avoiding A One-Way Orientation

As a demonstration of the ineffectiveness of ignoring feedback, try this exercise. Place paper and pencil before you, then blindfold yourself. Write your name and address in the upper right-hand corner of the page, then draw a map showing where your home is located. Note on the map any points of reference which would be helpful.

1. How did it feel to have no visual feedback? _____

_____

2. How accurate was your drawing? _____

_____

The situation could have been improved greatly if you had been able to see, if someone else had drawn for you while you described your location, or if someone could have given you verbal feedback as you drew. In other words, your message would have been a lot more effective if you had the active participation of a receiver. That is true of *all* communication.

•The Interaction (or Two-Way) Model of Communication. The second model of communication, more realistic than the first, recognizes the responses we get from others as important. The model looks something like this:

The interaction model says that communication is not just action; it is also reaction. It is not just stimulus; it is also response. A good communicator skillfully prepares and delivers messages, but also pays close attention to reactions, or feedback, from the receiver. To study communication, we need to study how people send and respond to messages.

Although this idea of interaction is an improvement over the action model of communication, it is still oversimplified. It describes communication as a linear process, one in which a message is sent and then feedback is received. One thing happens, then the next, and so on. This doesn't sound unreasonable until you try to identify stimulus and response or cause and effect in a recent conversation you had. Perhaps you greeted someone. What was the stimulus for the greeting? The other person's greeting? The look? Constraints of the situation?

Instead of being a response, was your greeting a stimulus to the other person's response? Or was it both? What caused you to say what you did? What the other person said? What you thought the other person's words meant? What you felt because of the words? What you felt because of the way the other person said the words? What you felt because of the way the other person looked when speaking? We could ask all these questions and more about the other person's next comment!

Can you distinguish the stimulus and response, the cause and effect? I can't.

Seeing communication as interaction is more accurate than seeing it as action, but it still isn't complete. Also, it isn't totally ethical (in the sense described earlier) because it doesn't rec-

6

ognize the complete interdependence of the sender and the receiver. I could fulfill the model by speaking a while and then asking, *Are there any questions?* (adding the feedback loop). But I might still feel like I did under the action model: that I am responsible to initiate the communication, that I am to be in charge, that I answer your questions in order to make my meaning known to you. I would not expect to try to learn your meaning or to be changed or to grow in the communication.

I may be either deliberately or unintentionally manipulative in making it seem as if I recognize the importance of your input when I really don't. In addition, I am limiting the range of my choices in the communication situation even as I opt to be responsible for the range of your choices. Unfortunately, many leaders operate in just this way, not because they are inherently manipulative, but because they have not explored beyond a two-way, interaction model of communication.

David's men demonstrated an interactive approach to communication. They approached Nabal, ostensibly asking a question. In reality, they were expecting a particular answer, one favorable to their request, and were unwilling to accept any other. When they received Nabal's negative feedback, they immediately went to David with the bad news. Let's look at Nabal's response. Though all of us would agree that Nabal was surly instead of gracious, he nonetheless had a legitimate concern: servants were leaving their masters, and he was afraid his servants would leave him, too. If David's men had been open to Nabal as a person with a variety of options in the communication situation, they might have been able to negotiate with him. If they had recognized that his response was based on a real concern, they might have helped him avoid what he perceived as negative consequences of their request.

Skill Assessment: Two-Way Communication

1. List three examples you have experienced when communication was handled as if it were merely two-way, or stimulus/response. _____

_____

_____

2. How do you feel when you are in a situation in which the other person treats the communication as if it were two-way, or stimulus/response?_____

3. Think of a time when you behaved as if communication were just stimulus/response. What happened? How did you feel? How did the other person feel?_____

_____

_____

Skill Practice: Interdependence

Try the following experiment to explore the interdependence of senders and receivers. The next time you are in conversation with a person with whom you feel safe, vary the ways you react to comments they make and then assess their reactions. For instance, if your friend tells you that she just found a wonderful bargain at a sale, look downcast or out the window as if you are bored. Probably this reaction will not be the expected one! Your friend may ask you what the matter is, or if you heard her. Or, she might ignore you in her excitement.

In any case, after a brief time, ask her what she thought of your reaction. Discuss the impact you each have on the other when you are in conversation. What are some of the signals you typically read from her in determining her moods or attitudes? Ask her what signals she gets from you. Consider the ways in which you influence each other regardless of whether you are the sender or the receiver of the message.

•*The Transactional Model of Communication.* The view of communication with the greatest ethical potential is the third point of view, transaction. I'll try to explain it by contrasting it with the action and interaction views of communication.

If one views communication as an action, the primary concern is with each individual's performancc. Communication is more than independent message-sending. If one views communication as interaction, there is a greater recognition of the full process. Obviously, this view emphasizes feedback, communication as a response to the other person, and how communication continuously involves mutual and reciprocal influence.

Communication is more than a linear stimulus/response. In psychological terms, a transaction takes place when all parts or aspects derive their existence and nature by participating in the event. Going beyond action and interaction, transaction indi-

8

cates that we construct our views of ourselves, of others, and of meaning as we communicate in relationship with others. A model of transaction would look something like this:

ELEMENTS:
Source
Receiver
Message
Feedback
Environment

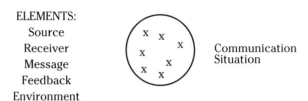

Communication Situation

Communication is between persons, and it is the *between* that a transactional view tries to recognize. To identify the *between*, a transactional view of communication takes into consideration four important elements.

First, communication is a *process*. Instead of trying to delineate a specific cause or beginning, transaction recognizes that communication is continuous. Our choices are influenced by elements of our past and present that we might not even be aware of. Any communication choice we make does not end once it is completed. It may have ramifications as communication continues. As human beings, we cannot specify cause and effect; we can simply point out interrelationships. We are constantly changing. A transactional view of communication highlights the dynamic nature of our interplay with others. We learn more about ourselves and others and continue to change with them as our communication continues.

Second, communication is a *Gestalt*, a totality depending on all our systems. Our internal systems (attitudes, emotions, understandings, background, psychological well-being, physical health, etc.) interface with our external systems (situation, time, place, urgency, ritual, etc.) to provide an opportunity to gain understanding. Understanding cannot come divorced from the mesh of our internal and external systems.

Each new communication situation is unique, then, for even if we could hold the external circumstances constant, we change internally as time passes. Because of what we have learned about ourselves and others in the interim, we view similar situations differently each time we are in them.

Third, communication is *perceptual*, creative. No two people

9

perceive the same event in the same way. Our frames of reference are necessarily different because of the differences in our backgrounds, information, interests, attitudes, etc. To the extent that our experiences are similar, we may tend to interpret events similarly. To the extent we differ, our interpretations probably differ.

Semanticists say that words have no meaning; only people have meaning. This statement implies that any word or verbal message will mean something different to each person hearing it. For example, take that sentence itself (words have no meaning; only people have meaning). I've said it countless times, and it means something fairly specific to me: a meaning of a word only occurs when a person assigns that meaning to the word; the word cannot fly into my head carrying meaning. But I don't know what that sentence means to you. One interpretation might be, *She's crazy; dictionaries are full of the meanings of words.* Another might be, *Ummm, words aren't significant then; people are significant.* Still another could be, *How can we ever manage to communicate?* Others might be saying, *I didn't get that at all. What did she say?*

The whole concept of connotation grows from this view. We have certain feelings about certain words, and those feelings amplify the meaning we assign to them. Meaning, then, is created out of individual perceptions. You cannot pass a meaning to me. I must assign meaning to the stimulus you provide.

Fourth, communication is *uncertain.* We can never predict exactly what will happen in a communication situation. What kind of response will I get, and how will I respond to it? What meaning will someone else assign to my message? What message might they send that will enlarge or change my perspective on a matter? Human beings do not provide exact responses to particular stimuli; we are unpredictable.

All four of these elements—process, totality, perceptions, and uncertainty—rest on the common assumption that human beings are choice makers. They recognize that we are all free to respond to any given stimulus in any number of ways.

Therefore, the view of communication as transactional is an ethical viewpoint, resting on the recognition of freedom of choice. This view indicates the inappropriateness of trying to structure someone else's choices. It points out the necessity of continuing communication with a person in order to learn to share meanings and come to mutually acceptable choices.

Abigail was a transactional communicator. She understood that this communication took place in an ongoing *process* of communication and could only be assessed in light of the relationship between David, Nabal, and their servants. She looked at the entire situation, its *totality*, and realized the inappropriateness of Nabal's response in light of David's expectations. She immediately tried to understand the message Nabal had sent from the point of view of David's men and knew that the *perception* David and his men would have of Nabal would be extremely negative. She considered Nabal's state of mind and knew that it was not the time to try to reason with him.

Finally, Abigail took action. Uncertain as to the outcome, she was willing to risk that in transaction with David, she could prevail upon his values and attitudes in such a way that he would eventually agree with her.

Have you seen leadership exercised in such a way that you felt your choices were limited by someone else and you were not allowed to express yourself fully? What happens when leaders behave as though they are responsible for the choices of everyone? There is a significant loss to the group if all attitudes, values, and insights are not explored. The danger may be as great as that incurred by Nabal, because such behavior puts the group at risk of dying or stagnating.

On the other hand, consider how you feel when your opinions are sought out, when someone listens to you and maybe even changes their mind, when you truly feel that you are connected and involved with another person. That is the goal of the transactional leader.

Skill Assessment: Transaction

1. List three examples of transactional communication you have experienced. _____
   _____
   _____

2. How do you feel when you are in a situation in which you are treated as a full partner in the communication? _____
   _____
   _____

3. Think of a time when you behaved as if communication were transactional. What happened? How did you feel? How did

11

the other person feel? _____
_____
_____

Skill Practice: Transaction

If you are studying this book in a group, try this exercise. Ask five volunteers to move to the front of the room. Ask the group to answer these questions about the volunteers:
1. Did they grow up in an urban area or a rural area?
2. Do they come from a large family or a small one?
3. How old were they when they first drove a car?
4. Would they rather vacation at the beach or in the mountains?
5. Would they rather make a speech or bake a cake?
6. What was their favorite subject in school?

Go back through each of the questions and ask for a show of hands on the answers chosen. Then ask these questions:

How did you decide on your answers? (Perception)

When did the messages start from the volunteers? (Process)

How did each of the volunteers communicate to the group? (Totality/Gestalt)

How much of what was communicated was deliberate and how much was unintentional? (Uncertainty)

If you are not in a study group, try this exercise with a new acquaintance. Each of you should answer the questions about the other then compare notes.

The ethics of communication have to do with our attitudes toward others in any relationship. Those attitudes determine the kind of relationship—and the kind of communication—we will have. To accept the other person and the range of choices, and in so doing to accept our own range of choice, that is the challenge for leaders as they demonstrate ethical communication.

Skill Evaluation: Ethical Communication

To assess your group's success in using ethical, transactional communication, use one of these evaluation procedures:
1. Ask everyone to fill out the evaluation form.
2. Select members at random to do an evaluation.
3. Spend time with the group collaboratively evaluating the communication of the group.

Evaluation Form

1. What was the most successful piece of communication at this meeting? Why was it so successful? _____

   _____

   _____

2. What was the least successful piece of communication at this meeting? Why was it unsuccessful? _____

   _____

   _____

3. What could have happened at the meeting to help you feel more respected and involved?_____

   _____

   _____

4. List one or two specific suggestions to improve the next meeting. _____

   _____

   _____

CHAPTER 2

Leadership: What It Is and How We Can Get Better at It

Deborah was a prophetess and a judge in the hill country of Ephraim. Israelites obviously trusted her for they came to her to have their disputes settled. For twenty years the Israelites had been oppressed by a cruel military commander, Sisera. Deborah sent for Barak from one of the towns particularly affected by the Canaanite oppression and gave him specific instructions to lead the way with ten thousand troops to Mount Tabor in order to engage Sisera in battle. Barak agreed to go only if Deborah would go with him.

Barak followed Deborah's instructions and defeated Sisera. Only Sisera himself escaped death and fled to the tent of Jael. She was married to a Kenite, people who were friendly with Jabin, the king of Canaan, so Sisera assumed she would be an ally. He asked for a drink, and she gave him both milk and a place to hide. When he fell asleep, Jael picked up a tent peg and a hammer, and drove the peg through his temple. (Her family, evidently, had previously been allied with Israel.) Deborah then wrote and sang a song of celebration for the great national victory (based on Judg. 4:4-5).

Deborah is a woman who demonstrates the very best principles of an approach to leadership called situational leadership. Taking into account the needs of the people she was leading, she changed her style in order to help them grow in the tasks she assigned them. Situational leadership, a model developed by Ken Blanchard and Paul Hersey, can give us guidance regarding the communication style to use in a given situation.

Leaders can be leaders, after all, only if their followers follow them! That means leaders must be carefully tuned in to the needs of their followers. If a leader meets a person's needs, that person will be extremely loyal. Too often leaders begin to think that followers are supposed to meet the leader's needs. And at that point, the leader will begin to lose strength as a leader.

Benjamin Disraeli said, "I must follow the people. Am I not their leader?" This funny twist of words has a significant message; in fact, leaders must *follow* the needs of their people.

There is no one perfect leadership or communication style. What is effective depends on the situation, the needs of the people involved, and the job the leader is asking them to do. The leader must assess the specific task in a given situation and determine the ability and the willingness of the individual or group being asked to accomplish it.

Ability. Is the individual capable of doing the task? Has she ever done it before? Has she been trained? If the answers to these questions are yes, the worker needs little information or direction from the leader. If the answers are no, the worker needs a great deal more communication in the form of attention and assistance from the leader.

Willingness. Is the worker confident of her ability to do the task? Is she comfortable with the assignment? Does she want to do it? If the answers to these questions are yes, the worker needs less encouragement and support from the leader than if any of the answers are no.

Remember that the ability and willingness of a person to do a task needs to be assessed with regard to each task faced. A person may be well prepared in one area, and woefully inadequate in another. The ability to do any one task changes over time.

Skill Assessment: Ability and Willingness

1. Think of a time when you were asked to take on a responsibility you had never done before. What was your first reaction?

   _____

2. What were your questions? What did you need from your leader in that situation? What kind of answers/support did you get? _____

3. Think of a time when you were asked to do a task you had done many times before. What was your reaction? _____

4. What kind of questions did you have? What did you need from your leader in that situation? What answers/support did you get? _____

Once the leader has diagnosed the ability and willingness of the individual or group to do a specific task, she then chooses among four communication/leadership styles.

LEADER SUPPORT

High — Encouraging | Coaching

Low — Delegating | Telling

Low   High

LEADER DIRECTION

1. *Telling.* When the individual or group has a low level of ability and/or willingness, the leader needs to give a lot of emphasis on the task. Be specific with instructions about what needs to be done, when it should be done, how it should be done, and who should do it. Stay in close touch; set up frequent reports or meetings. Provide manuals with detailed information, pair a new leader with an experienced one as a model, set timelines and deadlines.

Deborah functioned in a *telling* fashion when she first called Barak. She said very specifically, "The Lord, the God of Israel, commands you: 'Go, take with you ten thousand men of Naphatali and Zebulun and lead the way to Mount Tabor. I will lure Sisera, the commander of Jabin's army, with his chariots and his troop to the Kishon River and give him into your hands'" (Judg. 4:6-7).

Barak evidently felt very uncomfortable about taking on this task. He was either unwilling or felt unable to accomplish it alone. In fact, he said he would follow Deborah's instructions only if she went with him. Deborah recognized he would not be able to succeed alone and agreed to go with him (vv. 8-10).

2. *Coaching.* When an individual or group begins to develop a bit more experience and willingness, the leader can move to a style which is a little less directive and a little more supportive. A coach gives a great deal of direction about the task, but also

provides encouragement and support. Be there to encourage those you have asked to take on responsibilities; drop by before or after their meetings to give feedback and affirmation; set up planning and debriefing sessions which include celebration of successes.

Barak became more confident as he and Deborah were followed by ten thousand men. Deborah moved to a coaching style when she urged him, "Go! This is the day the Lord has given Sisera into your hands. Has not the Lord gone before you?" (Judg. 4:14). Barak needed no more specific instructions from her; he was ready to destroy Sisera's troops.

3. *Encouraging.* A group or an individual with a good bit of experience and willingness to do a task is usually eager to have a say in how the task is done. They do not need a great deal of instruction and supervision; they do need facilitation in moving into a leadership role of their own. Allow them to develop the specific ways of making something happen. Be available for assistance but leave direct implementation to them.

During the time of Jabin, the evil king of Canaan, Deborah was Israel's leader. My guess is that she used encouragement as a primary style of communication with her people. The people came to her for help in deciding their disputes (vv. 4-5). This sounds like she empowered them to be involved in those decisions. After the defeat of Sisera, she joined Barak in a song of great jubilation. She recognized her role in the triumph, but she also paid homage to others who were involved (Judg. 5).

4. *Delegating.* Truly experienced, capable, and eager individuals or groups are able to take on the responsibility of the task, leaving the leader to spend time on other tasks or with other groups who are at a lower levels of ability and willingness. Allow your leaders to be in charge unless they come to you with requests for assistance.

Jael is an example of a leader who was willing and able to take on a job by herself. Deborah knew from the first that Sisera would be defeated by a woman (Judg. 4:9), and was obviously willing to leave that entirely up to Jael. Jael was the wife of Heber the Kenite, from a clan which had become friendly with Jabin the king. Sisera clearly went to her because he thought she would provide a safe hiding spot.

However, she was true to her family's previous alliance with Israel, and had no hesitation in carrying out her plan to destroy Sisera. She invited him into her tent, an ideal hiding place, for no man other than a woman's husband or father was to enter a woman's tent. She gave him milk and, after he fell asleep, killed him by driving a peg through his temple. Capable of the task, she carried it out without direction or encouragement.

Skill Practice: Leadership Styles

Think of a situation in your group which calls for one of these leadership styles. Describe the situation, explaining why the particular style is appropriate in light of the willingness and ability of the followers in that specific instance. Explain specific actions you should take in that situation.

1. Telling: _____
   What will you do as the leader? _____
   _____
2. Coaching: _____
   What will you do as the leader? _____
   _____
3. Encouraging: _____
   What will you do as the leader? _____
4. Delegating: _____
   What will you do as the leader? _____

Skill Evaluation: Effective Leadership

Consider using the following evaluation instrument at the conclusion of each project your group completes. Group members involved should fill out individual evaluations. Use answers to help you plan the next event.

Task/Process Evaluation

1. Were the specific goals of this task clear? Yes ___ No ___
2. What specifically made the goal so clear or unclear? _____
   _____
3. Did you have an understanding of what you were supposed to do on this task? _____
4. What did the leader do that helped you? _____
   _____
5. What would you have liked the leader to do more of? _____

6. What would you have liked the leader to do less of? _____

_____

7. Did you receive encouragement and support in accomplishing this task? Yes ___ No ___
8. In what specific ways were you encouraged and supported?

_____

9. Next time, what would you suggest to help the leader improve? _____

_____

No leader is perfect, but the most effective leaders remember that people perform best when their needs are met. A good leader asks questions and listens carefully to assure that she can offer the direction and the support most needed by her team. She helps her followers do their very best by choosing the appropriate leadership style in any given situation.

CHAPTER 3

Interpersonal Communication: Perception Is Reality

Ruth and Naomi's relationship has served as a model of commitment through the centuries. Naomi and her husband left Bethlehem to live in Moab in order to survive a famine. Their two sons grew up there and eventually married Moabite women. As time passed, Naomi's husband and then her two sons died. Aware that the famine had passed, Naomi felt that her life as a widow would be better back in Bethlehem where she had kinfolk. Her two daughters-in-law, Orpah and Ruth, traveled part way with her before she urged them to return to their families. Eventually Orpah decided to do just that, but Ruth stayed with Naomi, maintaining her commitment to Naomi's family and to Naomi's God.

In Bethlehem, Ruth was regarded as a foreigner. Nonetheless, she offered to gather grain for their food. Her demeanor, hard work, and reputation for taking care of Naomi won her the admiration of Boaz, Naomi's wealthy kinsman who owned the field. In time, Naomi guided Ruth to claim the right that Boaz marry her in order to perpetuate the family line. He happily did so. Their child, cared for by Naomi, was Obed, the grandfather of King David (based on Ruth 1-4).

Why do two different people sometimes have great difficulty in communicating? And why do some people just immediately seem to see the world the same way? Our communication rests on our perceptions of each other and of the world around us.

Perception is a personal, individual process drawing on our experiences, attitudes, background, and values. No matter how much credence we give to eyewitnesses and first hand reports, those reports vary widely from each other. This is natural, for all people see the world from their own vantage point.

Think of the implications these widely differing perceptions have on communication. Sometimes I think it is one of God's great miracles that we can ever understand another person at all! It can help to have a basic understanding of how the process of perception works. Knowing its structure may help you identify a point at which your perception and that of another person may differ. It may also give you a way to avoid some misunderstandings or to clear up some misperceptions.

Perception

When we perceive something, at least four processes are occurring almost simultaneously. Let's look at each of them.

• *Selectivity*. We are never able to perceive all of any event.

Skill Assessment: Selectivity

Sit quietly for a moment. Try to identify everything that is happening in your environment.

1. What are the sounds you hear?_____

2. What do you see? _____

3. Have you considered everything in all directions? _____

4. What do you feel? (consider physical sensations and emotional ones) _____

5. What are the smells around you? _____

6. Now consider any other people in your immediate vicinity. What is each one of them doing, seeing, hearing, feeling, smelling, etc.? _____

In this assessment, you feel how overwhelming it would be to try to perceive all of any event. We select aspects of an event or situation to pay attention to. There will always be other aspects of which we are simply unaware.

How do we select what we perceive? Several factors influence our selection. For instance, there are *physiological factors* which impact our perception. Sometimes we cannot see or hear something clearly. Have you ever overheard a conversation in another room when you could hear parts of the discussion, but not all of it? Have you ever been seated behind a post or a very tall person at the theater? Have you ever been at one end of a block when you saw and heard a wreck at the other end of the block? In each case, your perception was limited because of physiological factors.

A childhood rhyme tells of six blind men who, by touch, were asked to describe an elephant. The man touching the elephant's side told of a wall; the one touching the tusk thought of a spear. The trunk was perceived as a snake, the knee a tree, the ear a fan, and the tail a rope. The rhyme concludes that while each was partially correct, all were wrong.

In addition to physiological factors, there are also *psychological factors* which influence what we select to perceive. In essence, we pay attention to those things which interest us. For instance, if you are driving down the street when you are very hungry, you will probably notice the fast food advertisements. You are interested in anything which says food! On the other hand, if you drive down the same street when you are not hungry, but when you are wanting to buy a new car, you will probably not notice the food signs at all, but you will notice the various makes, models, and colors of cars.

One time my husband and I were in the market for a new car. After deciding on just the make and model we wanted, we went shopping. There was a shortage of these cars at the time, so we were delighted to find just what we wanted on the showroom floor. It was the cutest little yellow car I had ever seen! In fact, I couldn't remember ever having seen a yellow car before. I was so excited because it was what we wanted and because it was so unique. Do you know that the next day as I drove to work, I was amazed to see how many yellow cars there were on the road! I had simply never been interested in yellow cars before, and now I was.

This same principle works in relationships. We often see what we are interested in seeing. If we want harmony, we will see it. If we are looking for a fight, we will see just those elements that justify the fight.

The third factor influencing how we select what to perceive is *past experience and learning.*

Skill Assessment: Past Experience

See if you can solve this familiar puzzle:

1. Connect all nine dots with four straight lines.
2. You may not lift your pen or pencil from the time you begin until you complete the puzzle.
3. You may cross lines, but you may not retrace a line.

You have probably seen this puzzle before. Can you solve it? If you can't remember how to complete it, check the end of this chapter for the answer.

Why is this a hard puzzle to solve? Usually, people see the dots as a square or a box. Consequently, they try to solve the puzzle by drawing the lines in a square. The puzzle can be solved only if you are able to see the dots in a different framework and draw your lines outside the limits of the box.

Perception works the same way. Consider how people who are trained differently might see an automobile accident. A doctor would see injured people in need of help; a mechanic would see damage to the car and a vehicle in need of repair; and a police officer would see possible violations of the law.

Have you ever been in the midst of trying to solve a problem when someone else, maybe unfamiliar with what you were doing, looked at your work, and said, "Why don't you try it this way?" and you suddenly realized they were right? Sometimes we are so familiar with something, so sure we know just how something works, that we are unable to find the creative answer which solves our problem.

Keep in mind that selectivity is not bad. In fact, as our Skill Assessment showed, it can be a positive way to help us focus, concentrate, or be more efficient. In addition, of course, it can also be the reason for inefficiency, missing important indicators, or completely different understandings of a situation.

When Ruth went to Bethlehem with Naomi, she was regarded as a foreigner from a despised people. In Bethlehem the people selected one of her characteristic to pay attention to . . . the fact that she was foreign.

Skill Practice: Dealing with Selectivity
Choose a situation which is important to you. Ask yourself the following questions to help yourself assess the situation more completely.

1. In what ways might you be physiologically limited in this situation? _____
   _____

2. How might you expand your physiological perceptions?
   _____
   _____

3. How are your particular interests influencing your perception? _____
   _____
   _____

4. Now choose a psychological frame of reference. How does this impact your perception? _____
   _____

5. What has been your training and experience regarding this situation? How is that influencing your selections? _____
   _____

6. How would you perceive this situation if you were:
   12 years old? _____
   95 years old? _____
   from another country? _____
   unable to speak English? _____
   the opposite sex? _____
   a non-Christian? _____
   a new Christian? _____
   your Mother? _____
   the person with whom you have difficulty communicating?
   _____
   Jesus? _____

•*Expectation.* Once we have selected those aspects of a situation to which we are going to pay attention, the next step in perception is that we begin to make some predictions, or base some expectations, on those things we selected.

Skill Assessment: Expectation

In the blank beside each word listed below, put the first thing that comes to your mind as an expectation about people with that characteristic.

Blondes: _____

Doctors: _____

Musicians: _____

Athletes: _____

Missionaries: _____

Preachers' kids: _____

WMU leaders: _____

Now go back and think of an exception to each of the expectations you just listed.

This process is what happens when we stereotype people. Stereotypes are nothing more than predictions about people based on a few, selected characteristics.

That does not mean that the process of expectation is bad; it simply means that we have to be careful not to get locked into a set of expectations. It means that we need to always remember that our perceptions are selective; we never have the whole picture. I saw this slogan on the sign outside a church recently: *Beware of half truths. You may have the wrong half.*

We can use the process of expectation in a number of positive ways as well as negative ones. Expectations can become self-fulfilling prophecies. If we expect the very best of ourselves and others, we often get it!

One of my favorite stories is from "The People, Yes" by Carl Sandburg. A stranger asked a native, "What kind of people live here?"

"What kind of people live where you come from?" was the reply.

"Oh, they are terrible folks who cheat, lie, and steal."

"That's about the same kind of people you'll find here."

A time later another visitor approached this same man, and asked the same question. The man replied with the same answer, "What kind of folks live where you come from?"

This visitor responded, "They are kind, friendly, decent law - abiding people."

"That's the kind of folks you'll find around here," the man replied.

With expectation, just as with selection, there are positive and negative aspects. Expectations help us plan our actions and reactions. However, they can limit our range of behavior or our attitudes more than is practical. Assess the expectations you have of yourself and others on a regular basis. Be sure that you are not falling into a trap of being too negative or jumping to conclusions based on too few characteristics. Check with other people to find out what they are expecting; then compare notes. Why might they be expecting something very different from you? If your expectations are similar, double-check to see if you have overlooked anything.

Ruth had the gift of expecting the best of herself and of others. She said that she would be committed to Naomi, and so she was. She expected to provide for Naomi by gleaning in the fields, and she did. She claimed her right to become the wife of Boaz, and he married her. She set a whole series of positive, self-fulfilling expectations and benefitted from them.

Skill Practice: Expectations
1. Identify a situation in which you are trying to be successful.
   _____
   _____

2. Describe what would be different about yourself if, in fact, you were successful in this situation. _____
   _____
   _____

   Pledge to yourself that for the following week you will behave in those ways you just listed. In other words, behave as if you were already successful. At the end of the week, assess the way you feel about yourself. You may have begun to achieve part of the success of the situation simply because you are behaving as if you were successful.
3. Identify someone you know who is feeling uncertain about his or her abilities at something._____

4. List three to five specific ways you can convey to this person that you expect them to be successful._____
   _____
   _____

5. Implement your list and watch for reactions. Does the person strive to live up to your expectations? Do they seem pleased by your attitude? _____

_____

_____

•*Emotional Reactions.* The first step in perception is to select characteristics or components to pay attention to. The next step involves expecting or predicting behavior and reactions. The third step in perception is an emotional reaction to those selections and expectations.

Skill Assessment: Emotional Reactions

For the following items, list briefly something you selected to pay attention to, something you expected, and then your emotional reaction or how you felt during the process of selection and expectation.

1. The Kennedy assassination:
Selection: _____
Expectation: _____
Reaction: _____

2. The birth of a baby:
Selection: _____
Expectation: _____
Reaction: _____

3. The marriage of someone you love:
Selection: _____
Expectation: _____
Reaction: _____

4. The death of someone you love:
Selection: _____
Expectation: _____
Reaction: _____

5. The first day of spring:
Selection: _____
Expectation: _____
Reaction: _____

6. A worship service:
Selection: _____
Expectation: _____
Reaction: _____

7. Prayer/devotional time:
Selection: _____
Expectation: _____
Reaction: _____

It is not possible to avoid some sort of emotional reaction to any situation we perceive. Some of our reactions are obviously a lot stronger than others. In any case, our emotions influence the totality of our reaction. Sometimes I agree with you because I like you. Sometimes I like you because I agree with you! And disagreement works the same way.

When our emotions are particularly strong, we need to be careful that we are not overcome by them. It is hard to continue loving someone when they are doing something that makes us very angry. However, that is what we are commanded to do! We know that Jesus Himself experienced the full range of human emotions; it is all right for us to feel them. Just remember, Jesus did not let Satan manipulate Him even when He was hungry, lonesome, and tempted. Our emotions can be a real part of our perceptions without becoming the overriding aspect of them.

Certainly Ruth must have felt fear as she left her home, and even more so as she faced the prejudice against her ancestry. She must have been hurt and angry. In the face of these strong emotions, Ruth nonetheless went into the fields each day and behaved in a way that won the admiration of those around her and the heart of Boaz. She did not deny her emotions, but she did not let them overwhelm her, either.

Skill Practice: Emotional Reactions

1. List the three things which make you angriest._____
_____
_____
2. How do you usually react when you are really angry?_____
_____
3. Now, while you are not angry, decide how you would like to react when one of the three things you listed occurs._____
_____

The next time one of your three anger-producing situations occurs, go ahead and feel the anger, but change your behavior. Try something different to see if it produces a better reaction.

Keep trying behaviors until you find those which cause the most positive results for you and for the others in the situation.

•*Interpretation.* We have to make sense for ourselves of what we are perceiving. The processes of selection, expectation and emotional reaction happen so quickly that we are usually unaware of them. We become aware at the point that we put it all together into some whole, or Gestalt.

Interpretation is not always easy. More ambiguity means a greater range of interpretations.Think back over the process of perception. At each step, very personal elements are at play. You select characteristics because of your own interests and background. You expect certain things because of your selections and because of your experiences with similar situations. You react emotionally because of a host of related elements. No wonder you may understand a situation in a completely different way from someone else!

The information in this chapter is not designed to cause everyone to perceive things the same way. It is designed to help you identify the spots where you may be differing with someone else. It may help you troubleshoot situations so that you do not end up in misunderstandings that cause problems. It should help you arrive at a fuller, richer understanding by sharing your perceptions with others. Use the Skill Evaluation below as you consider your interactions with others.

Skill Evaluation: Perception

In any given situation, when you want to be sure that you are understanding as fully as possible the situation and the perceptions of the other people involved, use the following questions to help you share perspectives. Each person should answer the following questions.

1. List the three things in the situation which seemed the most significant. _____

_____

_____

2. Identify the impact of each of these three things on the situation. Why they are so important? _____

_____

_____

3. What do you expect to happen as a result of the situation?

Why? _____

4. What kind of reaction do you expect of the other people
   involved? _____
   _____

5. How do you feel about the situation? Why? _____
   _____

6. How do you feel about the people involved in the situation?
   Why? _____
   _____

7. What does it all mean? _____
   _____

8. What do you plan to do next as a result of this situation? ___
   _____

With each question, share answers as fully as possible.
Explore the reasoning behind each one. Be open to the possibil-
ity of changing your perceptions as you go along. Try to see the
situation from each person's perspective. You may not agree
with each person, but try to at least understand why they perceive the situation as they do.

Ruth was perceived in a variety of ways. She was regarded as
a widow, a daughter-in-law, a foreigner to be despised, and a
woman to be admired. She was the same person all along, but
the selections, expectations and emotions regarding her
changed depending on the person doing the perceiving.

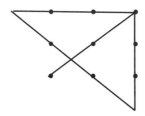

CHAPTER 4

Listening: The Creative Art

Mary, Martha, and Lazarus were like family to Jesus. It was to their house that He went for fellowship and rest. Martha, the elder of the sisters, took her responsibilities as hostess very seriously. Jesus brought His disciples with Him, so there were a number of people to feed and prepare for. She worked hard getting ready for them, and serving them after they arrived.

Mary was also excited about Jesus' visit. Her focus, however, was on the opportunity to be with Jesus Himself. She was so eager to be with Him that, even though women usually did not sit with men, she joined the group with Him in order to just listen to what He had to say.

After a time, Martha became frustrated with the responsibilities she had assumed and was shouldering alone. She went to Jesus, asking Him to tell Mary to help her. Jesus responded that Mary had chosen the better thing to do, to learn of Him (based on Luke 10: 38-42).

What do you think of when you hear people talk about the importance of communication? You probably think of people talking, then you may think of writing. Listening may not have even occurred to you as a part of communication. And yet, Jesus acknowledged that Mary's listening was the best thing she could do.

In fact, listening may be the most important part of communication. In a recent study, Joseph DeVito found that 45 percent of our communication time is spent listening. Other activities, in descending amount of time spent, are talking (30 percent), reading (16 percent), and writing (9 percent).

Think about a time when you were a student. How much time

did you spend learning to read, write, speak, and listen? My guess is that you spent the majority of your time learning to do the first three. Most of us spent a great deal of time learning to read and write. Some of us took speech classes or received some oral assignments. Very few of us have had any formal training in listening.

Yet, listening is not only the communication activity on which we spend the most time. More importantly, it is through listening that we validate each other. It is through listening that we create the opportunity to truly know each other. It is through listening that we learn understanding.

Skill Assessment: Importance of Listening

1. List the three best listeners you know and the characteristics of each. _____

   _____
   _____
   _____

   Do you dislike any of them? They are usually three of the people you like and respect the most. After all, they have shown the good judgement to pay attention to you!

2. List three of the worst listeners you know and the characteristics of each. _____

   _____
   _____
   _____

The Sperry Univac company built an entire marketing approach on its ability to listen well. Compare the characteristics you have listed with those identified in their listening training programs.

   Good Listeners: friendly, open, warm, empathetic, patient, honest, sincere

   Bad Listeners: closed, impatient, nervous, angry, unwilling to change

Good listening is critical to becoming a good leader. As we discussed in chapter 2, a leader must be aware of the skill level and willingness of people to do various tasks. Through good listening, a leader can have the information necessary to make wise decisions about how best to lead in a given situation.

In this chapter you will have an opportunity to assess your

own listening skills, identify some typical listening problems, and work toward increasing listening effectiveness.

Skill Assessment: How Well Do You Listen?

Take a few minutes to think about your listening skills. Instead of answering quickly or as you think you should, pause after each question to reflect on a conversation you had recently. Then answer as honestly as you can.

1. What were you thinking about as the other person was speaking?
2. Were you really hearing what the person was saying, or were you adding your own interpretation?
3. How do your attitudes about the speaker or the topic of conversation affect your listening skills?
4. How do hidden messages or unspoken communication affect the way you respond in a conversation?

Obstacles to Effective Listening

Let's look at a series of specific behaviors and/or attitudes which act as barriers to effective listening. There are simple ways to avoid or deal with each of the obstacles. As you read through the following list, try to think of times when you encountered each obstacle. What might you have done to correct the situation?

•*Focus on self.* Often during interactions with others, we are more concerned about what we are saying or going to say than what the other person is saying. Our thoughts fly ahead to plan our reaction to what is being said to the extent that sometimes we actually miss the comment to which we think we are responding!

Clear your mind and practice concentrating on the other person. Make an effort to send the impression that you are paying complete attention. It has been said that a *bore* is a person who talks when you wish him or her to listen; and *heaven* is a place where people do not tell you about their personal affairs, and listen attentively while you tell about your personal affairs.

•*Wandering mind.* The average speaker talks at a rate of about 200 words per minute. We are capable of thinking at a rate of about 400 words per minute. Consequently, there is a good bit

of mental time during which our minds might do a myriad of things other than concentrate on what the other person is saying. Try one or more of the following ideas to use the extra listening time effectively:
- •Outline what you are hearing.
- •Develop examples of the speaker's ideas.
- •Develop questions.
- •Mentally summarize what you have heard.
- •Apply what you are hearing to specific situations.

•*Leveling*. As we listen, there is often a tendency to simplify the message we are hearing in order to remember it better. That is the process of leveling. The problem is that we may omit details which are critical or which seem unimportant to us, thereby distorting the intent of the message.

Listen carefully to avoid leveling. You may wish to take notes in order to be thorough. Another strategy to avoid leveling is to compare what you heard with another person. Check to see if you are leaving out anything they felt was important. Of course, asking questions of the speaker, assuring that you have the message correctly, is always an excellent strategy.

•*Sharpening*. Certain things in a given message stand out over other things. We may know more or less about that particular topic, it may be more graphic, it may agree or disagree with certain attitudes or values we hold. When we pass the message on to someone else, the likelihood is that we will emphasize those particular points. We may even embellish them, and in the process, leave out other important information. That is the process of sharpening.

The strategies listed above for avoiding leveling are also useful for avoiding sharpening. You may wish to paraphrase the speaker's message and ask for feedback as to its accuracy.

•*Assimilation*. In this process, we tend to shape messages so that they confirm our own opinions or attitudes. The "spin doctors" we hear during political campaigns are examples. They are experts at making a message say what they need it to say. Sometimes we tend to assume that the other person's attitudes are the same as our own; therefore they must mean what we would mean if we were speaking.

Practice active listening. The more you try to listen from the other person's point of view, the more likely you are to understand their feelings and perspectives. Specifically ask yourself, *Assuming the speaker has the same beliefs that I do, what does this message mean?* Then ask, *Assuming the speaker has a different set of beliefs than mine, what could this message mean?*

•*Hearing what is expected.* Sometimes we are sure that we know what another person thinks or feels about an issue. We are so sure that we neglect to listen when they talk about it. And sometimes we are wrong! Be careful that you don't just hear what you expect to hear. Work at keeping an open mind. Actively try to think of two or three different perspectives the speaker might have. Celebrate surprises!

•*Passive listening.* Passive listening is the tendency to view the interaction as entertainment or as an event to which you are simply an audience. A passive listener tunes in and out, picking and choosing only parts of the message. Such a listener rarely develops a clear understanding of other people and their needs.

The antidote to passive listening is active listening. There are three simple strategies involved in being an active listener: paraphrase what the speaker is saying, respond to the feelings of the speaker, and ask questions.

Skill Practice: Active Listening

For each of the following situations, write out how you would paraphrase, respond to feelings, and ask questions.

Example: "I can't possibly take this position next year. I had that job once and it was a disaster. Nobody was ever willing to help, and I got stuck with doing almost all of the programs by myself."

Paraphrase: You had a very bad experience doing that job in the past because you did not have enough help.

Respond to Feelings: You must have felt really put-upon and alone.

Ask Questions: Would it make a difference this time if you had a co-chairperson?

1. I know I've missed a lot of meetings lately, but I've been busy, and besides, nobody called or anything so I didn't think anyone missed me.

Paraphrase: _____

Respond to Feelings: _____

Ask Questions: _____

2. Please don't ask me to pray at the meeting. I just can't pray in public.

Paraphrase: _____

Respond to Feelings: _____

Ask Questions: _____

3. I'd like to contribute to the missions offering, but what I can give is so little that it won't make any difference. Besides I don't even know who or what I'm giving for.

Paraphrase: _____

Respond to Feelings: _____

Ask Questions: _____

•*Missing the meaning.* There are several ways that we typically miss the meaning a speaker intended. I am reminded of a phrase we often hear: "They just don't get it." One of the typical problems is concentrating on the content of the message but neglecting to think about the feelings behind it. A second problem is evaluating or judging the speaker or the message before working for full understanding. The third barrier is to be too literal and thus miss more subtle or hidden meanings.

Try to listen for clues about the speaker's intentions and feelings. When you hear a comment, ask yourself *Why is the speaker saying that? What attitude or emotion may be behind it?* Think about relationship messages as well as content messages. What is the message saying about how the speaker feels about you? What are the implications of the message? What assumptions are under the message?

Be sure to defer judgement until you have heard the entire message and double-checked to be sure you understand its intention. Only then do you have sufficient information to begin to draw some conclusions.

Ten Tips for Effective Listening

Brenda Ueland suggests ten steps we can take to improve our listening skills.

1. Stop talking! As long as you are talking, you cannot be listening.
2. Behave as you think a good listener should behave. For

instance, here are several things a good listener might do:

a. Put the speaker at ease. Set up a good environment for talking and listening. Remove distractions.
b. Show you are interested. Establish good eye contact. Give nonverbal signals that you are paying attention.
c. Be patient. Give the speaker plenty of time.
d. Don't react emotionally. Keep concentrating in an effort to understand the message even if you do not agree with it.

3. Listen for the main points. Building a mental outline can be helpful. Take notes if that helps you. Develop in your own mind the central message of what you are hearing.

4. Concentrate. Keep your total focus on the person speaking. In the book *Stranger in a Strange Land,* by Robert Heinlein, one of the characteristics which most endeared the alien to people on earth was his ability to concentrate totally on the person with whom he was interacting.

5. Be open-minded. Don't make up your mind in advance about what the speaker will say or how you will react to it. If you are hearing something with which you disagree, pretend you are a debater who must argue both sides of the issue. Do your best to gather any information which refutes your original point of view. Then assess the conflicting ideas carefully to determine where you want to stand on the issue.

6. Watch out for words which elicit emotional reactions from you. We all have signal reactions to certain words. Words like Baptist, Republican, Democrat, Fundamentalist, Liberal, missionary, offering, and numerous others call forth a habitual response — we always react the same way when we hear them. Identify those words for yourself and slow down your reactions to them. Think about why you react that way. Force yourself to get past the words in order to understand the person speaking them.

7. Defer judgement. Wait until you have heard and are sure you understand the entire message before you make decisions.

8. Listen empathetically. Try to assume the speaker's point of view as you listen. Seek to approach the message from the other person's perspective instead of your own.

9. Ask questions. Questions show your interest and encourage the speaker. They also clarify the message for you.

10. Stop talking! This is the first and the last of the techniques

for effective listening. Instead of thinking about how to impress people with your wit and wisdom, plan to support others by your careful attention to them. Think about what the other person must be feeling as you listen.

Skill Practice: Supportive Listening

Use a strategy developed by Carl Rogers which is often used in counseling and other forms of therapeutic listening. When you are in conversation with someone, require yourself to paraphrase what the person has said and get confirmation from them that you are correct, before you allow yourself to make your own comments.

Mary was a listener who instinctively knew the techniques of good listening. She was quiet, responsive, and supportive of Jesus as He spoke and taught. We know that her entire focus was on Jesus, even to the point of forgetting the norms of the times and her responsibilities as a hostess. And we know that she listened well and absorbed His meaning, because Jesus commended her.

Skill Evaluation: Are You an Effective Listener?

At the conclusion of an interaction with someone, ask yourself the following questions. Then ask the other person to assess your listening skills by answering them as well.

1. Did I listen more than I spoke? Or did I speak more than I listened? What was the ratio of listening to speaking? _____

2. Did I put the other person at ease? What did I do to improve the listening environment? How did I show nonverbal support for the speaker? _____

3. What were the main points of the speaker's message? _____

4. Did I concentrate on the other person and their message? What did I do to help my concentration? _____

5. Was I open-minded? What was my initial point of view on the subject? What is it now? What did I learn? _____

6. What were the emotions I felt as I listened? Were there any

words or ideas that usually serve as flash points for me? How did I handle them? _____

7. Did I defer judgment? How did I make sure I understood the message before I came to a decision about it?_____

8. How did I show empathy? What was the point of view of the speaker in this message? How did I develop an understanding of the speaker's perspective? _____

9. What questions did I ask to help me better understand the message? _____

Nonverbal Messages: The Art of Unspoken Communication

Dorcas lived in Joppa, a seaport city about 34 miles northwest of Jerusalem. As a part of an active Christian community, she evidently provided a great deal of leadership in reaching out to minister to the poor. She was known as someone who was always doing good.

Dorcas became sick and died. Those who loved her prepared her body for burial and placed her in an upstairs room. Then they heard that Peter was in Lydda, not too far away. Immediately they sent for him, asking him to come at once. Whether they wanted him there because they thought he could perform a miracle, or because he should be there for the burial, we don't know. We do know that Peter went right away.

When Peter arrived at the upstairs room, it was filled with widows, who showed him the robes and other clothing Dorcas had made. After sending everyone out of the room, Peter knelt and prayed. Then he turned to Dorcas and asked her to rise. She opened her eyes and sat up. Peter called everyone back in and presented Dorcas to them. This event became known all over Joppa, and many people believed in the Lord (based on Acts 9:36-41).

Dorcas witnessed nonverbally as she gave of herself to others. Her giving was so unstinting that she was an example to many, both in her own time and in ours. Without words, she preached the message of Jesus Christ and set the example for Dorcas Societies worldwide, clothing and caring for people in need. Expressions such as *Actions speak louder than words*, or *What you are doing speaks so loudly that I cannot hear what you are saying*, or even *Faith without works is dead*, all imply the significance of nonverbal communication.

Researchers in the field of communication claim that nonverbal communication, such as the ways words are said and facial expressions, relay more information than do spoken words. R.L. Birdwhistell, a noted researcher, estimates that 65 percent of meaning in a conversation is communicated nonverbally. Albert Mahrabian, another researcher, estimates the percentage to be 93 percent: 38 percent the way words are said; 55 percent facial expression; and only 7 percent verbal.

Nonverbal communication, anything other than the spoken or written word, covers a host of forms of communication. In fact, it involves so many things that it has been said that we cannot *not* communicate. Think about that for a minute. Even a refusal to communicate communicates something!

Often our nonverbal communication is unintentional. Have you ever had someone come up to you and ask, *What's wrong?* You weren't intending to convey distress, but something about your expression sent that signal. Our clothes, the condition of our desk and office, our housekeeping style, the appearance of our yard, the time we spend in certain activities — these are all ways we communicate whether we intend to or not. Our Christian witness is often the product of unintentional messages. These can be the strongest messages we send!

In this chapter, we will be looking at the functions of nonverbal communication and at a variety of forms of body language.

Skill Assessment: Nonverbal Communication

Try the following exercises to begin determining the importance of nonverbal communication for you.

1. Watch a conversation from a distance. Based on facial expression, body language, and tone of voice (if you can hear the sounds of the voices), make up what you think the content of the conversation is. What are the attitudes of the people involved?_____

2. The next time you are in an intense conversation, try to answer these questions:
   a. What does the other person's facial expression indicate to you? _____
   _____

   b. What is your facial expression and what does it communicate? _____
   _____

   c. Watch the other person's body language. What does it indicate about the attitude? _____
   _____

   d. What is your body language indicating to the other person? _____
   _____

   e. How would you describe the sound of the other person's voice? What reaction do you have to it? _____
   _____

   f. How does your voice sound? _____
   _____

   Now try a different tone of voice and watch for reactions.
3. Make a list of all the activities you participated in last week. Based on the amount of time spent, determine which activities are the most important to you. _____
   _____
   _____

Functions of Nonverbal Communication

Nonverbal communication can function in at least three different ways. First, and most frequently, it augments verbal communication. We expect gestures to go along with what someone is saying. We laugh that some people would not be able to talk at all if their hands were tied behind their backs! We use gestures and tone of voice to emphasize ideas, to show emotion, to make something funnier.

Secondly, we may use nonverbal communication instead of verbal communication. Sometimes we are unable to talk (for example, when someone else is speaking, we don't know the language, we don't want to be heard, or we are underwater). We nonetheless convey messages in a number of ways. There are formalized ways of using nonverbal communication to replace verbal. For instance, sign language with the deaf is a complete language of its own. Television studios and underwater divers have full sets of signals to convey important information.

A third form of nonverbal communication contradicts the verbal message. Usually the contradiction is unintentional, though often humor or sarcasm deliberately use this strategy to make a point. When there is a contradiction between verbal and nonverbal messages, which do you think is more important? That may be a hard question to answer in the abstract. Consider this: your best friend comes running up to you with a huge smile, gives you a great bearhug, and says, *I could just kill you!* Do you feel threatened? Probably not. You would probably tune in to all those positive nonverbal signals and assume that your friend is being very affirming, perhaps about to chastise you for some particularly nice thing you have done.

Here is another example. What if your spouse refused to look you in the eye, hung his head, shrugged and turned away from you, and said in a lackluster voice, *You know I love you.* Would you feel confident and secure in his love? Probably not, because these nonverbal behaviors send negative messages. If a verbal message and a nonverbal message contradict each other, we almost always will believe the nonverbal message.

Consider Dorcas and the nonverbal messages she sent as she sewed for those in need. Did her messages augment her verbal witness? Did they substitute for spoken messages? Or did they contradict her other messages? We don't know a lot about Dorcas' verbal interactions with others. We do know that her behavior spoke for itself. She was known for always doing good. Her behavior complemented her Christian commitment, and it may well have stood on its own as a substitute for more assertive forms of witness. In no way did Dorcas' behavior contradict the Christian principles by which she lived.

Skill Practice: Functions of Nonverbal Communication
Experiment with some of the following ideas.

1. For a set period of time, rely entirely on nonverbal messages. Make notes of your feelings. _____

_____

_____

2. Think of various ways to augment your verbal messages. Consciously try a different tone of voice. Plan a visual aid. Experiment with facial expressions and gestures. _____

_____

_____

3. In your mirror at home, practice a variety of ways to contradict a verbal message you are planning to deliver. Then try delivering it nonverbally. Based on those experiences, determine the best ways to use nonverbal communication to augment the message. _____

_____

_____

_____

4. Assess the nonverbal messages at a WMU (or other) meeting. What messages are being sent without words? _____

_____

_____

What messages are being strongly reinforced with a nonverbal component? _____

_____

Do you see any contradictions? How do you interpret them?

_____

_____

Forms of Nonverbal Communication
Because nonverbal communication is so much a part of all our interactions with others, let's look briefly at the varieties of forms in which it occurs.

•*Body Language.* Body language is probably the first thing that comes to mind when we think of nonverbal communication. Consequently, it carries significant levels of meaning. Five specific types of body language can be identified to help us make choices about the messages we send and the meanings of the messages we receive.

1. *Emblems* are nonverbal behaviors which stand for an idea or a word. They can be translated directly and can easily substitute for the spoken thought. Examples include a wave, a hitchhiker's thumb, or praying hands. We are generally quite conscious of emblems both as we use and receive them.

2. *Illustrators* go along with the spoken word and help a receiver understand it by providing a visual demonstration of it. Measuring the length of something with our hands, pointing to something, or pacing out a distance are all examples of illustrators. Again, we generally are conscious of our use of this type of body language.

3. *Affect displays* are facial expressions which show an emotional reaction or state. Studies show that people in general are very good at reading emotional reactions. Sometimes our facial expressions are unintentional, and we give away clues to our inner feelings. Other times we intentionally use facial expressions to convey our feelings.

4. *Regulators* are used in conversations to monitor or regulate the flow of the discussion. We signal through facial expressions, posture, and gestures our reactions to what someone is saying, encouraging them to either continue or to stop and let someone else have a turn. Our indications of interest may include nodding our head, making eye contact, leaning forward, or other reactions showing our attention. These encourage a speaker to continue. Nonverbal indications that someone should stop talking may include a refusal to establish eye contact, drumming one's fingernails, or looking at a watch.

5. *Adaptors* are behaviors which indicate an inner state. Usually, they are an unconscious response to a need (like scratching an itch) or to relieve some emotion (rubbing your neck when under stress). We tend to interpret them unconsciously as well. Unless the adaptors are extreme, we tend to process them without really being aware of them.

•*Space Communication.* The way we place ourselves in relationship to others conveys a great deal about our feelings toward the other person, and about our cultural norms. In the United

States we tend to operate as if we were within a protective bubble of about 18 inches to four feet. When we allow someone within that bubble, we are signalling that we trust and/or care about that person. The more formal our relationships, the more distance we put between ourselves.

This use of space is absolutely tied to our culture. In other countries, people relate at completely different distances from each other. We do not touch each other much unless we are in a fairly intimate relationship; however, in other countries, there is a great deal more touching.

Missions outreach to other cultures demands that we study carefully to determine which behavior is appropriate and which is not. Our purpose is not to impose our own culture; we must learn to appreciate the culture where we are ministering.

•*Time Communication.* Time is another dimension which is bound to culture. There are at least three ways we use time to communicate. The first is *formal time*, those aspects of time which we establish in our culture as meaningful. We use seconds, minutes and hours. In other cultures, the significant units may be phases of the moon or seasons.

The second way to use time is *informal time*. We establish some rather inexact ways to refer to pieces of time and come to some sort of general agreement as to what they mean. For instance, we say *awhile*, *in just a second*, *a long time*, and *as soon as possible*. These units of time provide opportunity for misunderstanding even within our own culture because they are inexact. It is even more difficult to learn the informal units of time in another culture.

The third form of time communication is *psychological time*. This refers to the significance we place on the past, present, and future. That may vary from individual to individual, or from group to group within a culture. It certainly varies from culture to culture. Some Indian tribes see time as an ongoing flow within which they participate.

•*Artifactual Communication.* Not all nonverbal communication comes from our behavior. Some of it comes from the objects we use or with which we surround ourselves: the way we dress or accessorize ourselves, the type house we choose, the cars we drive, and so forth. A great deal of emphasis has been given in rocent years to dress, especially in professional contexts. All artifacts we choose say something about us.

Additional forms of nonverbal communication include the use of our eyes and our voices. These topics will be addressed in chapter 6.

Skill Practice: Forms of Nonverbal Communication
1. At the next meeting you attend, observe different types of body language. Watch for each of the following and identify the message you think they are sending.
Emblems:_____

_____

Illustrators: _____

_____

Affect Displays: _____

_____

Regulators: _____
Adaptors: _____

_____

2. Consciously attempt to use regulators which encourage a speaker. Watch for and record the reaction. _____

_____

3. Visit with someone from a different culture or with a missionary who has served in another country. Explore the differences they experience in the use of space and time.
Space: _____
Time: _____
4. Assess your own use of time. What messages are you sending with the way you spend your time? _____

_____

What messages are you sending with the way you use another's time? (For example, are you frequently late to meetings? Do you do reports on time?) _____

_____

Skill Evaluation: Nonverbal Communication
Next time you are planning a presentation, a conversation, or a meeting, ask someone in the audience, or one of the receivers, to do the following nonverbal assessment for you.
1. What did my voice convey about the message and my feelings about it?_____

_____

2. How should I try to improve my voice?_____

_____

3. What did my body language convey about me and/or the message? _____

_____

4. How could I improve my body language? _____

_____

5. What did my clothing, accessories, etc. convey about my message and/or about me? _____

_____

6. How can I improve my dress, accessories, etc. to convey a more positive message? _____

_____

_____

Dorcas sent significant messages through her behavior to people who knew her. She gave to others, she did for others, she cared about people in need. Her life served as a witness to her faith and spoke more loudly to those around her than anything she might have said. Our behavior also communicates. Learning to send nonverbal messages which speak truly of our inner efforts to live our faith is a worthy attempt. Remember to witness nonverbally as well as verbally.

CHAPTER 6

Public Presentations: The Confident Speaker

Miriam, a leader and prophetess, was the first woman patriot and first woman singer on record in the Bible. She was introduced as a child of about seven, standing watch over Moses, her infant brother, in a basket in the bulrushes. When the Egyptian princess rescued the baby, Miriam thought quickly and offered to find a Hebrew woman to nurse him. Miriam's wit and her willingness to approach the princess to offer her help allowed Jochebed, Moses' and Miriam's mother, to raise her son in the Egyptian palace.

Though the Bible doesn't tell a lot about Miriam's life after that incident, we know that she grew up loving God and believing His promise to protect the Hebrews and make a great nation of them. Her leadership skills must have been formidable, for the prophet Micah preaches of God's care of the Hebrews by saying, "I brought you up out of Egypt and redeemed you from the land of slavery. I sent Moses to lead you, also Aaron and Miriam" (Mic. 6:4). Miriam was fully a partner in Moses' release of the captives.

Miriam confidently led the song of celebration when God brought His people safely through the Red Sea. With her tambourine, she led others to sing and dance as she proclaimed, "Sing to the Lord, for he is highly exalted. The horse and its rider he has hurled into the sea" (based on Ex. 15:21).

Miriam, who must have been persuasive, models for us the characteristics of an effective speaker. She had a message to deliver, and she was able to involve the people in her song.

Do you like to make speeches? Some people do, but many others would avoid making a speech at all costs. A survey a few years ago revealed that for many people, the fear of speaking before a group was greater than fears of height, financial problems, deep water, sickness, and dying. When some people say, *I'd rather die than give a speech*, they are telling the literal truth!

Nonetheless, the ability to speak articulately and persuasively before a group is one of the more important skills a leader needs. In this chapter, we will work on the following basic skills for increasing your confidence as a public speaker: dealing with speech apprehension, using nonverbal strategies, and focusing on the audience.

Speech Apprehension

The usual term for nervousness before an audience is stage fright. That term, however, implies that fear is present. Now think a minute about how you feel when you are nervous about speaking. Are you actually *afraid* of the audience or the situation? Do you really *fear* that they are going to do something harmful to you? Probably not. What you are feeling is actually the very normal reaction of a conscientious person who wants to do a good job. Your concern, a normal desire to be successful, is over the quality of your effort.

Because of that, speech teachers have begun using the terms speech apprehension or speech anxiety to refer to those feelings before giving a speech. Fear occurs when there is a real, external stimulus. Anxiety usually relates to internal qualities rather than external events. A person is afraid of a criminal; they have anxiety about their ability to fit in at a new job.

All of this is to say that you are really not scared about public speaking; you want to do your best. And that is good! The tips to follow about dealing with anxiety will not eliminate it; they will help you deal with it. I hope you never get rid of some level of speech apprehension. That means you take your responsibility to an audience seriously and want to do your best. Celebrate that! Enjoy the added energy and enthusiasm that comes from your apprehension of the situation.

Skill Assessment: Apprehension Questionnaire

For each statement, indicate the response that seems most appropriate for you. These responses should be your first impressions and not how you think the ideal communicator would respond. Indicate your responses on a scale of one to five (1=strongly agree; 2=agree; 3=undecided; 4=disagree; 5=strongly disagree).[1]

_____1. While participating in a conversation with a new acquaintance, I feel very nervous.

_____2. I have no fear of facing an audience.

_____3. I talk less because I'm shy.

_____4. I look forward to expressing my opinions at meetings.

_____5. I am afraid to express myself in a group.

_____6. I look forward to an opportunity to speak in public.

_____7. I find the prospect of speaking mildly pleasant.

_____8. When communicating, my posture feels strained and unnatural.

_____9. I am tense and nervous while participating in group discussion.

_____10. Although I talk fluently with friends, I am at a loss for words on the platform.

_____11. I have no fear about expressing myself in a group.

_____12. My hands tremble when I try to handle objects on the platform.

_____13. I always avoid speaking in public if possible.

_____14. I feel that I am more fluent when talking to others than most people are.

_____15. I am fearful and tense the entire time I am speaking before a group of people.

_____16. My thoughts become confused and jumbled when I speak to groups.

_____17. I like to get involved in group discussions.

_____18. Although I am nervous just before getting up, I soon forget my fears and enjoy the experience.

_____19. Conversing with people who hold positions of authority causes me to be fearful and tense.

_____20. I dislike using my body and voice expressively.

---

[1]From McCrosky, James C. and Wheeless, Lawrence R., *Introduction to Human Communication*. Copyright © 1976 by Allyn and Bacon. Adapted by permission.

_____ 21. I feel relaxed and comfortable when speaking.
_____ 22. I feel self-conscious when I am called upon to answer a question or give an opinion in a group.
_____ 23. I face the prospect of making a speech with complete confidence.
_____ 24. I'm afraid to speak up in conversation.
_____ 25. I would enjoy presenting a speech on a local television show.

To Score: Compute your score in the following way:

1. Add up your scores for items 1, 3, 5, 8, 9, 10, 12, 13, 15, 16, 19, 20, 22, and 24: _____
2. Add up your scores for items 2, 4, 6, 7, 11, 14, 17, 18, 21, 23, and 25: _____
3. Complete the following formula to find your Apprehension Score: 84 - _____(total from Step 1) + _____(total from Step 2)

To Interpret Your Score: Scores of 88 or higher would indicate considerable apprehension. Scores between 75 and 87 would indicate some apprehension. Scores below 74 would indicate little apprehension.

Another way to think about speech apprehension is to understand it as a normal reaction to a potentially threatening situation. Our bodies are prepared to deal with a threat by either running away or fighting. You have probably studied this tendency called *fight or flight.* In other words, when we feel speech apprehension, we can be assured that our bodies are preparing in the most efficient way possible for us to be at our best. Our muscles tense for agility, our heartbeat and breathing increases to provide more fuel, our glands secrete fluids to sharpen our senses and give us energy. This process is a great gift from God! Unfortunately, most of the time when we become aware that our hearts are beating faster, our breathing has increased, and our muscles are tense, we think, *Oh, no! I'm scared!* What we should be thinking is, *Wonderful! My body is operating at top condition. I am ready for anything!*

The only difficulty is that when we are in a public speaking situation, we really are not supposed to fight or to fly away. We have to stay right there, looking completely under control with our bodies revved up like crazy! We experience symptoms of nervousness because our bodies are ready to do something extremely active, yet we are standing still. Think for a moment about your own nervous symptoms.

Skill Assessment: Nervous Symptoms

What do you feel when you are nervous? Assess the feelings you are most aware of in a public speaking situation:

1. *Voice* (quivering, too fast, too slow, monotone):_____
2. *Verbal Fluency* (stammering, halting, vocalized pauses [such as "uh"], speech blocks): _____
3. *Mouth and throat* (swallowing, clearing throat, heavy breathing, dryness): _____
4. *Facial expression* (lack of eye contact, eyes everywhere, tense face muscles, twitches, blushing): _____
5. *Arms and hands* (rigid, tense, fidgeting, shaking hands, hands in pockets or hair, sweaty palms): _____
6. *Legs and feet* (swaying, shuffling feet, pacing, knocking knee):

_____

If you look back at your various symptoms, you can see that almost all of them are examples of your body trying to work off the excess energy it has generated. If your hands or legs tremble, your muscles have tensed in preparation for action. Try holding your arm out in front of you, elbow bent, and tense your muscles as hard as you can. Your arm will begin trembling. That is what is happening when you have speech apprehension. If you have a sinking feeling in your stomach, it is because your body is generating adrenalin and other glandular secretions. When that happens, the process of digestion stops and your stomach contracts, causing the sinking sensation.

You can see why it is not practical to talk of eliminating the symptoms of speech apprehension. Your goal should be to control those symptoms. Glenn Capp tells of a student in a speech class who said, "When I first started taking speech, I could hardly talk for shaking. Now after taking ten courses, I have learned to talk while shaking."

Controlling Speech Apprehension

Here are some tips for controlling speech apprehension.

1. Know your own reactions. Look back at the list you developed in the Skill Assessment on Nervous Symptoms.
2. Develop a plan for dealing with each symptom. For instance,

if you have trouble with your voice, practice breathing exercises. If your palms sweat, keep a handkerchief in your pocket. If your mouth gets dry, have a glass of water handy.

3. If you have trouble with shaking hands or legs just before speaking, work off the excess energy. If possible go somewhere private to do some physical exercise before you give a speech. Swing your arms, jog in place, do knee bends, rotate your neck and head. These exercises will use up some of the tension which gathers as your body prepares for fight or flight. You'll be surprised at how much more in control you feel of your physical reactions. If you are unable to hide to do exercises, try isometric exercises just before speaking. Tense your muscles as hard as you can, and then release them.

4. Care about your audience. Instead of thinking about yourself and how you are doing, consciously think about the audience. Watch them to see if they are interested. If not, do something to spice up your speech. Look at the audience's facial expressions to see if they seem to be understanding you. If not, explain more fully, or ask them what may be confusing them. If you convey that you really care about your audience members, they will respond positively to you and your message.

5. Develop some good memory aids. Do not write out your speech word for word. If you do, you will be tempted to read it, and a speech that is read to an audience is usually dead. Speak from an outline, but feel free to make notes on it, to draw arrows or stars to remind you of important points, or to underline or use colors to make it easy to glance down and find where you are.

6. Do some preliminary work to reduce any worries you may have. Give yourself plenty of leeway to arrive on time. Look around you; become familiar with the environment. Dress in something that is comfortable and makes you feel good. Meet some people ahead of time so that you look at friendly faces as you speak.

7. Practice, practice, practice. Nothing helps your confidence more than knowing what you are going to do and say. Practice aloud; you sound differently aloud than you do in your head. Practice with a mirror so you can see your facial expressions and body movements. Practice with a video camera if you have access to one, or at least with a tape recorder

so that you can hear how you sound. Practice with your family and friends; ask them for feedback.

8. Seek out opportunities to give speeches or to make presentations before groups. Your skill and confidence will grow with the added experience.

9. Remember, you are engaged in God's work. He is there to support you. Think how nervous Miriam must have been when confronting the Egyptian princess, but she did it, and God used her in the process.

Nonverbal Strategies

Eye Contact. Probably the most important thing you can do as a speaker is to establish good eye contact with your audience. This accomplishes at least three things: first, it allows you to show that you care about your audience; second, it gives you the opportunity to observe their reactions so that you can modify your presentation if necessary; and third, it conveys the message that you are a credible speaker.

Skill Practice: Eye Contact

Try this exercise when you are speaking to a group. Establish eye contact with a single individual and maintain it for five seconds before you move your eyes to look at someone else. Five seconds will seem like an eternity, but it is a reasonable time to convey that you really are speaking with the person you are looking at. As you change eye contact, move across the room in a zigzag, or Z shape, so that all parts of the room are covered. Continue to spend five seconds in contact with each person.

Voice. The next important part of your speech is the sound of your voice. *How* you say what you say carries more meaning than the words themselves. In chapter 5, we discussed that the sound of your voice alone carries up to 55 percent of the meaning you convey. In addition, speakers who are dynamic and who have vocal variety are thought to be more credible than speakers who speak in monotone. Both the increased rate of speaking and the increased pitch variety convey a sense of animation and dynamism.

Sometimes nervous speakers tend to withdraw vocally, their voices becoming timid and quiet. It is almost as if they think people won't really notice they are speaking at all if they speak quietly and without expression! In truth, that very retiring manner of speech calls attention to itself, saying *I am boring, not interested in what I have to say, not really interested in you and whether you care about what I am saying.* Those are negative messages you don't want to send.

If you have a tendency to speak this way, work hard to overcome it. The first tip is to care about what you are talking about. If you are really committed, enthusiastic, and care about your audience, it will show in your voice. You cannot care passionately about something and speak in a monotone.

The second tip is to add stories, examples, and instances to your presentation. When people tell a story, they usually get more energetic vocally. You will, too, if you have prepared your speech with a number of interesting examples.

The third tip is to listen to yourself on a tape recorder. Assess what you like and what you do not like. Decide if you could enjoy listening to yourself for an extended period of time. If not, make some changes. There are three primary vocal characteristics you can control:

1. *Pitch.* Though the length of your vocal folds determines how high or low your voice is pitched, it is possible to make some changes. In general, a very high pitch conveys uncertainty, immaturity, and a lack of substance. If your voice is high-pitched, you can lower it a tone or two by consciously practicing and listening to yourself.

Skill Practice: Pitch
1. Count to five in your normal speaking voice.
2. Begin again at that same pitch, but lower your voice a tone on each number as you count to five.
3. Count to five again, beginning at your normal tone, and raise your voice a pitch with each number.
4. Read the following passage from the song sung by Miriam, Moses, and Aaron. Follow the changes in pitch as indicated to impact the meaning.

(*Normal*) I will sing to the Lord for He is highly exalted.
(*Lower*) The horse and its rider He has hurled into the sea.
(*Normal*) The Lord is my strength and my song; He has become my salvation.
(*Higher*) He is my God and I will praise Him,
(*Normal*) my father's God, and I will exalt Him (Ex. 15:1-2).

2. *Pace.* Some people naturally speak more slowly or more rapidly than others. Dialectical differences in some parts of the country influence our speaking rate. Nonetheless, we can learn to control the pace of our speaking. No one likes to listen to a constant, unchanging speaking voice. If you tend to speak slowly, be aware that a fairly rapid rate of speech sends the message that you are more animated, that you are more interested in your audience, and that you are more credible. Those are characteristics worth working toward! It is better to speak a little too fast than too slowly. The main thing to strive for is variety in your pacing. Use a change in pace to signal a change in subject, or to let your audience know that something significant is about to be said.

Skill Practice: Pace
1. Watch the clock and speak as quickly as you can to see how far you can count in five seconds.
2. Now see how slowly you can count and still sound normal. At that rate, how far would you count in five seconds?
3. Read the following passage about the deliverance at the Red Sea, changing rate as indicated. How does the rate change impact the meaning?

(*Very slow*) Your right hand, O Lord, was majestic in power.
(*Slow*) Your right hand, O Lord, shattered the enemy.
(*Normal*) In the greatness of Your majesty You threw down those who opposed You.
(*Faster*) You unleashed Your burning anger; it consumed them like stubble.
(*Faster*) By the blast of Your nostrils the waters piled up.
(*Slower*) The surging waters stood firm like a wall;
(*Slower*) The deep waters (*even slower*) congealed (*a little faster*) in the heart of the sea (Ex. 15:6-8).

3. *Inflection.* Say the following sentence aloud: *I would not say we lost the fight.* Now varying the inflection, continue to say the sentence aloud:
I would not say we lost the fight.
I would not *say* we lost the fight .
I would not say *we* lost the fight.
I would not say we *lost* the fight.

61

I would not say we lost the *fight*

The words remained the same in each sentence, but the meaning changed as you changed the inflection, or emphasis you placed on the words. Inflection is one of the most important tools you have at your command.

Inflection is made up of a variety of elements. The force with which you say a word, the tone of your voice as you say it, the pitch variations you use, and your rate are all a part of inflection. Good speakers use these elements to capture interest.

Skill Practice: Inflection

1. Speak the sentence, "He did that," and suggest the following different meanings: ask a question; shock; delight; sarcasm.
2. Say "Hello" in a variety of ways to express: warmth; surprise; disgust; shame.
3. Read the following passage from Miriam's song with variety and expressiveness. Try it two or three different ways.

"The enemy boasted, 'I will pursue, I will overtake them. I will divide the spoils; I will gorge myself on them. I will draw my sword and my hand will destroy them.' But you blew with your breath, and the sea covered them. They sank like lead in the mighty waters" (Ex. 15:9-10).

Audience and Situation Analysis

Audience Analysis. People have three choices of focus in a public speaking situation.

1. They can focus on the content of what they want to say in their speech. This is called message-centered communication. The content is important; speakers should not waste an audience's time with less than the best they have to offer in the way of ideas and information.
2. They can focus on themselves, how they are saying what they are saying. This speaker-centered communication is important, too, for speakers should be at their best for an audience. They should know their content and be comfortable in their delivery.
3. They can focus on the audience, how their message is being received by the listeners. This is called audience-centered communication, and it is the most important of the three approaches. A speaker caught up in the other two approaches can neglect the audience. Sometimes speakers

can be so polished that they offend an audience or seem too aloof. Sometimes a message can be too esoteric or erudite for the audience. But a speaker who thinks of the audience first will adapt to the needs of that particular group of people. A speaker who really cares about the listeners and shows it is way ahead in terms of focus.

Start by finding out what your audience knows about your topic. If you are talking about mission work in Bolivia, you should know whether your audience knows where Bolivia is! Perhaps someone in the audience has been there, or is familiar with the same kind of work in a different place. The more you know about your audience's knowledge of the topic, the better able you are to determine your level of speaking. You will be able to give relevant examples, and you will be able to ask audience members to help you out with examples of their own. Don't embarrass yourself by talking only about those things which an audience already knows, or which are so difficult that the audience cannot understand them.

The next thing you need to know is your audience's attitude about your topic. Are they excited about it? Did they come specifically because of the topic? Are they there because they are concerned and want to give a perspective counter to yours? Don't let yourself get blindsided by attitudes you didn't know were there! I once represented the city I worked for when I gave a speech to an organization of homebuilders. I went without finding out that they were furious with the city because of some recently passed building regulations. It did not matter what I was there to talk about; they were set to oppose anything the city was in favor of! I should have known ahead of time so that I could have diffused some of that anger. At the very least, I would not have been caught off-guard.

Next, ask yourself what the audience knows about you. Do you share something in common with them on which you can build? If you are not known, it is always appropriate to be introduced, and it is also appropriate to provide information for the introducer. Be sure to include things which will be of particular interest to that specific group of people.

Finally, try to find out as much as you can about the people making up the audience. Ask the person who has asked you to speak to give you information about them. Find someone who knows someone in the group and ask questions. Get to your speaking engagement early and meet some people so that you can find out about them through your conversation.

Skill Practice: Audience Analysis
Before you speak to a group, learn the following:
1. What does this audience know about your topic? _____

_____

2. How do they know that? _____

_____

3. What is their attitude toward your topic?_____

_____

4. What does your audience know about you?_____

_____

5. In what ways are you like your audience? _____

_____

6. Find out the following characteristics about the majority of those to whom you will be speaking:
   age: _____
   sex: _____
   race:_____
   family status: _____
   economic status:_____
   employment: _____
   education: _____
   politics:_____
   religion:_____

Situation Analysis. I once went to conduct a workshop at a conference of hospital financial managers, thinking I was to speak for one hour to 400 people. I arrived the night before the speech to discover that I was to speak three hours to 40 people! Needless to say, I got little sleep that night while I frantically adapted my presentation.

A few questions ahead of time will save you untold embarrassment later. Here are some things you should find out from the program planner or person in charge of the situation:

1. *Date and Time:* Is there anything special about the day? Does the time of day have any impact: will the audience be sleepy, tired, or hungry?

2. *Size of Audience:* How many people will be there? Are they there voluntarily?

3. *Place:* Will you be inside or outside? How will the room be arranged? Will there be a speaker's platform or lectern? Will you need a microphone? What equipment for visual aids is available?

4. *Type of Meeting:* What kind of meeting is this? Why are they meeting? What is likely to be the general mood or atmosphere?

5. *Kind of Program:* What is the agenda? Will there be other speakers? When are you on the program? What else is happening both before and after your speech?

Skill Evaluation: Confident Speaking

After a presentation, answer the following questions to assess your development as a confident speaker.

1. How did you feel before you gave the speech? _____

_____

2. What did you do to handle your symptoms of apprehension?

_____

_____

3. How well did it work? What will you do next time?_____

_____

_____

4. Assess your use of eye contact. Ask someone in the audience how they perceived your use of eye contact. _____

_____

5. Grade yourself on a scale of one to five (five being the best) on the following aspects of making a presentation.
   _____ a. Vocal variety
   _____ b. Dynamic rate
   _____ c. Comfortable pitch
   _____ d. Interesting inflections

6. How did you go about assessing the audience. How effective were you?_____

_____

_____

7.What did you find out about the audience that you didn't know?_____

_____

8. How did you find out about the speaking situation? What will you do next time to be sure that all information is available?

_____

_____

Miriam knew her audience and its situation well. She was able to capture the mood and involve them in her song of joy. Seek, in all your speaking, to focus on your audience and let them help make your speech a success.

CHAPTER 7

The Message: Making It Meaningful

Priscilla and her husband Aquila were tentmakers. They were also Christians with a burning missionary drive. As Jews ordered to leave Rome, they welcomed Paul to stay in their home when he left Athens and went to Corinth. Paul, also a tentmaker, felt comfortable with them. He stayed in Corinth for a year and a half, preaching and working with his friends. When he left to go to Ephesus, Priscilla and Aquila sailed with him.

After a time, Paul left them in charge of the church in Ephesus. Their home became the meeting place for the group of Christians. One night, a brilliant young man named Apollos taught in the church with great fervor. After Priscilla and Aquila took him under their wings, teaching him more fully the truths of Christianity, he was able to go on to win many followers to Christ. Before, he had been drawing them to himself.

After the death of Claudius, who had ordered the Jews out of Rome, Priscilla and Aquila returned there. In Paul's letters to the churches at Rome and Corinth, as well as in his letter to Timothy, he mentions Priscilla and Aquila with great fondness and credits them with saving his life (based on Acts 18; I Cor. 16:19; Rom. 16:3; II Tim. 4:19).

These brief pieces of information about Priscilla imply a great deal more. In a society in which women were second class citizens, she is consistently mentioned before her husband. Her name is found on monuments in Rome. Tertullias, a Roman historian, mentioned her as "the holy Prisca, who preached the gospel." One of the oldest catacombs in Rome, the Coemeterium Priscilla, was named for her as was a church, Titulus St. Prisca. Tradition credits her with a book, the *Acts of St. Prisca*, and some even credit her with the authorship of the Epistle to the Hebrews. She was, without doubt, a woman able to effectively and persuasively develop a message.

We have spoken about developing skills as a confident speaker. Now we concentrate on developing the message. The process is the same whether the message is spoken or written. The critical elements are purpose, organization, and support.

Purpose

It has been said that if you don't know where you are going, you may wind up somewhere else. Lewis Carroll, in *Alice's Adventures in Wonderland*, captures it perfectly when Alice asks the Cat which way she should go. Cat replied that it depended largely on where she wanted to go. When Alice said that she didn't much care where she went, Cat told her, "Then it doesn't matter which way you go. You're sure to get somewhere if you walk long enough." A clear purpose for any effort you make at communication is critical. If you don't know what you want to accomplish, how can your listener have any hope of getting there with you?

The five major purposes for a written or spoken piece of communication are to inform, persuade, entertain, inspire, and call to action. It is often difficult to completely separate these from each other, but for clarity, let's look at them one at a time.

1. *To inform.* Almost every attempt at communication involves informing. This is the keystone upon which the other purposes build. In order to inform someone, a communicator must make the message easy to understand, easy to remember, and easy to use. Critical strategies are good audience analysis, relevance to the audience's interests, and careful organization of information. The goal is a meeting of the minds, a sharing of understanding on the topic at hand.

2. *To persuade.* Some argue that all communication is ultimately persuasive. While that is probably true, we can generally define a persuasive piece of communication as one designed to convince someone to do or to believe a specific thing. The critical strategies are relevance to a felt need, credible support, and demonstrable benefits. The goal of persuasion is to

move an audience from where they are to a new spot, literally or figuratively.

3. *To entertain.* Communicating to entertain involves helping an audience relax and enjoy themselves, forgetting themselves in the process. Sometimes entertainment is humorous, but not always. A dramatic, well-told story can also move an audience beyond themselves. The critical strategies are understanding the audience, avoiding offensive material, and responding immediately to feedback. The goal is to help the audience escape from reality.

4. *To inspire.* This kind of communication is actually a subset of persuasive communication. It is unique, however, in that it asks for a higher degree of devotion or involvement than other forms of persuasion. In most cases, the critical strategies are to heighten attitudes and/or values which already exist. The goal is to call the audience to greater enthusiasm and to fulfill the commitments they have already made.

5. *To call to action.* Again, this is a form of persuasion, but it is only successful if it results in a specified action. The key is that the action is clearly delineated. The critical strategies are establishing a need, outlining an action in response to the need, showing how the action solves the need. The goal is to move the audience to immediate, specific action.

There is no question that Priscilla had a clear purpose in mind when she taught, wrote, or preached the gospel. Her purpose was to inform all who would listen about Jesus Christ and to persuade them to take Him into their own hearts and lives. Her work with Apollos is an example of her ability to craft a message to meet the needs of her audience.

Skill Assessment: Communication Purpose

1. Think about your last meeting. What did you talk about at the meeting?_____

_____

What was your purpose? _____

_____

Were you aware of the purpose at the time? _____

_____

Did you accomplish it? _____

_____

How and/or why?_____

2. Choose an article in your church newsletter. What is its purpose? _____

   Identify some specific strategies used to accomplish the purpose. _____

   Is the article successful?_____

When you are preparing to communicate, be very specific with yourself about your purpose. Sometimes we think vaguely that we want to persuade someone, but we do not clearly specify exactly what the end result of the persuasion will be.

A vague purpose statement would be: My goal is for the audience to be convinced that missions education is important.

Now consider these more specific purpose statements:

•My goal is for the audience to fund and staff a missions education program for our young people.

•My goal is for the audience to increase their giving to the current missions offering by 25 percent.

•My goal is for the audience to attend our mission study on Eastern Europe.

•My goal is for the audience to know that there is a missions education program for each age group in our church.

The more specifically you state your goal to yourself, the better able you are to plan and develop your communication.

Skill Practice: Accomplishing Your Purpose
Before your next effort at writing or speaking, answer the following questions:

1. Why are you doing this? _____

2. What is your relationship to the audience? _____

3. Does this communication need to inform, persuade, entertain, inspire, or call to action?_____

4. What is the specific response you hope for from the audience? _____

70

5. In one sentence, state the specific purpose of this communication. _____

Organization

Think of the last speech or sermon you heard. Can you outline it in your mind? If not, you are probably having difficulty remembering it at all! A carefully organized presentation is always easier to remember than one which isn't organized. The side benefit is that it is easier for you, the speaker, to remember as well. You will feel much more comfortable delivering a well-crafted message than a loose, rambling one.

As you put a presentation together, think of the following three aspects of organization: organizational patterns, development of ideas, and order.

•*Organizational Patterns.* Your goal as you put your presentation together is to accomplish your stated purpose. Since all of the purposes we discussed above involve either informing or persuading, let's look at several patterns specifically designed to accomplish these purposes. When you have to make a presentation, simply choosing an appropriate pattern will help you organize your thoughts and communicate with your audience.

To inform:
1. Chronological or historical: Organize the main points of your presentation by time. Describe events in their order of occurrence. If you are giving instructions, tell what to do first, second, third, etc.
2. Climactic: Save the most dramatic or exciting information for last. of your presentation Use the first part of the presentation to build to the climax.
3. Comparison and contrast: Divide the speech into two sections. In one section, explain the similarities between two ideas, situations or circumstances; in the other, develop the differences.
4. Definition: Divide the term being discussed into its component parts. Use denotative and/or connotative definitions. For instructions, use operational definitions.
5. Geographical/spatial: Organize information by location.

Describe an area from east to west, top to bottom, etc

6. Topical: Divide the topic into its major components, describing them in whatever order makes sense.
7. Multiple Patterns: Any patterns above can be combined.

To persuade:
1. Cause to effect: First develop the causes of a situation, then explain the effects.
2. Effect to cause: Explain the results of a situation. Then explain what caused it.
3. Deductive: After stating a conclusion or generalization, develop arguments to support it.
4. Inductive: Explain a series of arguments or ideas and then draw a conclusion based on them.
5. Problem-solution: Describe a problem. Offer a solution or a plan to solve the problem.
6. Elimination: Describe a problem. List all the possible solutions and then show that all solutions have problems, which would eliminate all but one.
7. Reflective: Describe a problem. Suggest several solutions, evaluating the merits of each one. Based on the relative merits, recommend one of the solutions.
8. Motivated sequence: This pattern has been shown to be particularly effective in helping people follow reasoning to a conclusion. It has five steps:
   a. Attention: call attention to the problem.
   b. Need: relate the need to the interests of the audience.
   c. Satisfaction: offer a solution.
   d. Visualization: describe the benefits and advantages of the solution.
   e. Action: describe what the audience should do to accomplish the solution.

•*Development of Ideas.* Keep your audience in mind as you work with your materials for your presentation. You want to be sure that they find your information clear, interesting and memorable. Outlining is an excellent strategy for trouble-shooting your plans for the presentation. The basic structure to follow in an outline is:
   I.   Introduction
   II. Body

III. Conclusion

It is always easier to deal with the body of the presentation first. That is, after all, the meat of the matter. After you know *what* you are going to say, it is usually a simple thing to develop how to introduce and conclude it. We will deal with introductions and conclusions in the next section. Right now, let's work on organizing the body of a presentation.

You have probably heard the old saying that a sermon should have three points and a poem. That is a good pattern to follow for any presentation. In other words, determine the three (more or less) most important things you need to say and then begin to support them. Here is a suggested way to structure each of your main points:

a. Statement of main point

b. Explanation/definition of terms

c. Evidence, examples, other materials

d. Restatement of main point

e. Transition relating this point to the following one.

Transitions are extremely important. As you outline, carefully plan how you will move from the introduction to the body, from each of the main points in the body to the next main point, and from the body of the speech to the conclusion. These are points in your presentation when you have opportunities to be sure the audience is understanding you, to assist them in following your reasoning, to remind them of important information, and to help them remember the critical information.

You may wish to use some of the following strategies to help make the transitions between points in your speeches:

a. *Transition words:* also, likewise, in addition, therefore, finally, on the other hand, although, because, since, in other words, for example.

b. *Questions:* Use questions to highlight what you just said, or to lead into the next thing you will say. Some examples of transitional questions are: Why are we talking about ___? What is significant about that? How does this affect us? Who should care about this? When will this happen?

c. *Repetition:* Use transition as a chance to repeat main ideas. For instance, you could say something like this: "I told you there are three reasons we need to participate in this project to feed the hungry. I told you about the first reason, that the greatest pocket of hunger is within six blocks of our church. I told you about the second reason, that we as a church need to grow by reaching out to help those in need. Now let's look at the third and most important reason, that this ministry will give us the opportunity to witness for Christ."

Skill Practice: Development of Ideas

Use this template as a reminder of the elements you want to consider as you plan your presentation.

1. What is your purpose statement?_____

   _____

   Is it primarily informative or persuasive?_____

   _____

2. What organizational pattern do you plan to use? _____

   _____

3. Outline the body of your speech following the pattern below: (This sample outline is merely a pattern. You may have more or less information related to any given main point.)
   - A. Main Point
     - 1. Explanation/Definition
     - 2. Evidence/Examples
       - a. Example
       - b. Statistics
       - c. Story
     - 3. Transition (restatement, etc.)
   - B. Main Point
     - 1. Explanation/Definition
     - 2. Evidence/Examples
     - 3. Transition
   - C. Main Point
     - 1. Explanation/Definition
     - 2. Evidence/Examples
     - 3. Transition

•*Order.* The most important parts of any presentation are the beginning and the end. At the beginning, you are making a first impression, and the audience is fresh and willing to listen. At the end, you have the opportunity to make a lasting impression with the final words the audience hears. Research has shown over and over that those two spots are critical.

In other words, when you plan the body of your presentation, put your most important information in the most important spots. You may wish to assign priorities to each of your main ideas, then put the most important one first and the second most important one last. The less important ideas go in the middle. Or you can decide to put the most important idea last, and the next most important one first. The less important ideas still go in the middle.

The first and last of the body of the speech are important; so are the first and last of the entire speech. The introduction and conclusion of a presentation are critical. Let's look at each.

•*Introduction.* A speaker needs to accomplish three things in the introduction: get the attention of the audience, establish rapport, and lead into the body of the speech.

There are several fairly standard techniques for introducing a speech. You may wish to use one, or a combination.
- •Quotation
- •Startling Statement
- •Story or Illustration
- •Personal Reference
- •Connection between speaker and audience
- •Compliment
- •Humor

Regardless of which strategy, or strategies, you use, be sure it will accomplish your three reasons for an introduction.

•*Conclusion.* A conclusion has two major goals: to wrap up/summarize your speech; to stimulate your audience to remember you, the speech, and or the action you need them to take. The strategies for conclusions are similar to those for introductions:
- •Summary
- •Story/Illustration
- •Quotation
- •Humor
- •An Appeal
- •A Challenge
- •A Call for Action

Skill Practice: Introductions and Conclusions
Double-check the introduction and conclusion of your next presentation by asking yourself the following questions:
1. What strategy(ies) are you using in your introduction? _____

2. In what way does this strategy(ies) fulfill the three major responsibilities of an introduction?

Get attention: _____

_____

Establish rapport: _____

_____

Lead into the body: _____

_____

3. What strategy(ies) are you using in your conclusion? _____

_____

4. In what way does this strategy(ies) fulfill the two major responsibilities of a conclusion?

Summarize/Wrap up the speech: _____

_____

Help the audience remember you: _____

_____

_____

remember the speech: _____

_____

_____

remember the action to take: _____

_____

Forms of Support

I once heard, *Some people speak in order to express their thoughts; others speak in order to cover up their thoughts; and still others speak instead of thinking at all!* If you want to express your thoughts, you need to spend some time considering the ways your audience will best understand them. Some people think visually; some think auditorily. Some people like a lot of factual, objective information; others like comparisons and abstract thinking. Some people like a lot of stories and examples; others want statistics and quantitative data.

Once again, it is critical to know your audience so that you can choose the information which will best communicate to them. Even so, there will be differences among the people to whom you speak. Therefore, use a variety of forms of support for your ideas. Some kinds of support will make sense to one group of people, and other forms will be meaningful to another group. That is fine. Just be sure to build into your presentation different and varied forms of supportive information, and you will eventually communicate with everyone.

•*Types of Amplification.* What are some of the ways of supporting or amplifying your main points? In the practice outline above, each main point was supported by explanations, definitions, evidence, and examples. Let's look at a variety of ways you can meet your audience's need to understand your message. The following is a list of the forms of support.

Analogy or Comparison. Show the similarities between something the audience knows and that which you want them to know. Comparisons may be literal, or they may be figurative. Be sure that your comparisons have more in common than they have differences.

Definition. A clear understanding of terms is necessary for communication. There are several ways you may define a term:

a. Authority: relying on an expert opinion.
b. Denotation: the dictionary meaning.
c. Etymology: the history of the term.
d. Model: show the actual item or a model of it.
e. Negation: telling what the term being defined is not.
f. Operational: explaining or showing what the term being defined does.

Examples. Use a story to illustrate a point. The story usually refers to something familiar, it adds spice and color, it appeals to emotions or personal needs, and it adds interest. There are at least three kinds:

a. Illustration: a long example.
b. Instance: a short example.
c. Hypothetical: an imaginary or symbolic example. Be sure your examples are relevant and are sufficient to make the point.

Statistics. Statistics are numbers or quantities used to make or to clarify a point. Be sure that your figures are recent and accurate, and from a reliable source.

Testimony. Quotations from a credible source can be used as testimony. You may quote someone directly, or you may paraphrase. Be sure that you are not misquoting, that you have not taken a statement out of context, and that you give the qualifications of the person you are quoting. Try to choose someone who will be automatically respected by your audience.

Skill Practice: Forms of Support

When you are preparing your next presentation, identify the main points as indicated above and then try using one or more of the following:

1. Practice amplifying each point with three different forms of support.
2. Ask a friend to give you ideas for different forms of support for each main point.
3. As you go through your presentation, ask audience members to offer forms of support for your main points.

Visual Aids. Another extremely important way to support or amplify an idea is through the use of visual aids. If at all possible, try to include something visual in every presentation. These aids can help you accomplish one or more of the following: reinforce the verbal message; stimulate interest; illustrate ideas which are difficult to visualize or imagine. Any time visual aids help an audience understand you, they are good. If they ever become the focus of the speech rather than its support, they may be getting in the way of real communication.

There are a number of visual aids, some of which include:

Audio-Visual Equipment. Use equipment such as an overhead projector, slide projector, film projector, video equipment, audio recorder, chalkboard, whiteboard, flip chart, etc.

Graphs. Computers make it easy to create such graphs as bar graphs, pie charts, and line graphs. There are also libraries of pictures to use.

Models. Actual models or even symbolic models can help you demonstrate the way something works.

Actual Objects. Show souvenirs, hobby materials, equipment, clothes, etc.

Below are some practical guidelines for using a visual aid effectively:

- It should be large enough to be easily seen by the entire audience.
- Be sure the aid supports your verbal message and doesn't substitute for it.
- Don't introduce the visual aid until you are ready for it. Put it away when you are through with it. Otherwise it will detract from what you are saying.

•Keep your focus on the audience and not on the visual aid.

Skill Evaluation: Making the Message Meaningful

Periodically, use the following evaluation form to test the effectiveness of your message. Ask your audience to fill it out and return it to you.

1. What was the purpose of this presentation? _____
   _____

2. On a scale of one to five (five being best), please rate how well the purpose was accomplished. _____
   _____

3. What did the speaker do in the introduction to capture your attention?_____
   _____

4. What were the three main points of the presentation? _____
   _____

5. List one piece of information or support for each of the main points._____
   _____

6. What was the most memorable part of the presentation? Why?_____

7. How does the speaker want you to respond to the presentation? _____
   _____

8. What will your response be? _____
   _____

9. What did the conclusion of this presentation accomplish for you as a listener? _____
   _____

10. Rate the effectiveness of the entire presentation on a scale of one to five (five being best). _____

Priscilla opened her home to provide a place for people to worship. When necessary, she traveled far away from home to spread the gospel. Her message was all-important, and she worked carefully to be sure it reached an audience. Priscilla is an example to us of a communicator who was committed to helping her audience understand the message of God.

Women of God: Leaders and Communicators

Abigail, Deborah, Ruth, Mary of Bethany, Dorcas, Miriam, and Priscilla were all women who used their talents in the service of God. All had magnificent talents; all were leaders. Central to the leadership each demonstrated was her communication skills. From quiet Dorcas to fiery Miriam, from insightful Abigail to impulsive Mary, these women communicated their commitment in their own unique ways.

You also have talents to be used by God. You are a leader in a variety of ways: at home, with friends, in your community, in your church, in your small group, etc. You often may not even realize when you are providing leadership. You are always communicating. Everything you do says something about who you are and your relationship to God.

Remember that effective leadership and communication involve skills that must be learned and practiced; they do not happen automatically. Use the skill exercises in this book to help you grow and develop. Use the skill evaluations to assess how you are doing as you apply your skills in various situations. Involve others and work together to improve the ways you interact with each other.

My prayer is that this book will help you feel and become more effective in the variety of ways you communicate and lead. You are a woman of God, gifted to serve. May you use your skills and talents in His will.

Group Study Guide—2½ hours

Use the skill explanation, assessment, practice, and evaluation in each chapter to plan a 2 1/2 hour study of this book. All participants will need a copy of the book.

Introduction: 15 minutes
Begin the study by asking participants to explain the statement, "You cannot not communicate." Then allow a few minutes for participants to suggest why it is essential for a leader to develop the skill of communication.

Study: 2 hours
Ask seven people to prepare a 15 minute study of one of the chapters. Encourage them to use the skill assessments, practices, and evaluations in the study. If you have fewer than seven participants, some may be assigned two or more chapters. Caution presenters that they must stay within the 15 minute time frame for each chapter. Use the additional 15 minutes for participants to respond to the presentations.

Conclusion: 15 minutes
Review the study by asking these questions: What new ideas about communication did you learn from this study? What communication skills will you begin now to improve or develop? Encourage participants to set definite skill improvement goals.

For a one hour study, ask participants to read the book and complete all activities. During the hour, briefly review each chapter, spending more time on those chapters that participants want to discuss.

Church Study Course
Communications Skills is course number 03386 in the subject area: Christian Growth and Service. Credit for the course may be obtained in two ways: (1) conference or class—read the book and participate in a 2½-hour study; (2) individual study—read the book, do the personal learning activities, and have a church leader check written work.

Request credit on form 725 Church Study Course Enrollment/Credit Request (rev.) available from the Church Study Course Awards Office, 127 Ninth Avenue, North, Nashville, TN 37234.

Complete details about the Church Study Course system, courses available, and diplomas offered is in the Church Study Course Catalog available form the Church Study Course Awards Office.

Communication Skills is one of five books in the *Leadership Skills for Women* series. These books are written *by* women *for* women as each exercises her God-given gifts to advance His kingdom.

OTHER BOOKS IN THE
Leadership Skills for Women series

Name _____

Address: _____

City: _____ ST ___ ZIP _____

Daytime phone # _____

Code #	Title	Qty.	Cost	Total
W923125	*With A Servant Heart*		$3.95	
N933105	*Relationship Skills*		$5.95	
N943116	*Time Management Skills*		$5.95	
N943117	*Conflict Management Skills*		$5.95	
N943115	*Communication Skills*		$5.95	
N933107	*Group Building Skills*		$5.95	

**Alabama Sales Tax	*Shipping & Handling		
8% Birmingham	0- $15.00 $2.50		Subtotal
5% Jefferson County	$15.01-$50.00 $3.25		**AL customers add tax
6% Shelby County	$50.01-$100.00 $4.00		*Shipping & Handling
4% Other Alabama	$100.01-& up $5.00		TOTAL ENCLOSED

Send to:
New Hope
P. O. Box 12065
Birmingham, AL
35202-2065

(205) 991-4933

**Order will arrive in
four to six weeks.**

PAYMENT MUST ACCOMPANY ORDER
☐ Check ☐ VISA ☐ MasterCard
PLEASE DO NOT SEND CASH

CARD NUMBER

EXPIRATION DATE

4 DIGIT BANK CODE
(MasterCard Only)

Authorizing Signature

M94NHLDS